'This is a wonderful account of the extraordinary life of Maud Kells, whose journey to ans

County Tyrone to Buckin

Republic of the Congo. Not

into Maud's deep persona

remarkable personality.

With each page, we learn more about her tremendous courage, compassion, and her good humour. No wonder this book is such a compelling read. If you are looking for an inspirational book, then look no further than An Open Door. *It recounts the life of a truly exceptional woman.'*

Lady Hermon, MP

'As a student I read some of Helen Roseveare's work and was always challenged by her bravery. Her books inspired me to work overseas, but the DRC I experience most days – air-conditioned offices in wealthy suburbs – is so very different from that of most Congolese that I always find it helpful to read of "real life" here. Maud's book gives us a real flavour of Congolese life.

Before moving to DRC I lived in Nairobi and used to enjoy Bible Studies with Jim Strait and his wife. I've enjoyed reading about Jim's "other life" rescuing people like Maud from difficult circumstances. MAF continue to be instrumental to our own Embassy work supporting humanitarian relief and healthcare programmes around DRC.

I've been reading this autobiography during the immediate post-electoral period here in DRC in January 2019. The government has shut down the internet and rumours abound. Who knows what the future holds? In this context it's been inspiring to read of Maud's work in DRC over many, many years and through many cycles of conflict and recovery and to know that, ultimately, God is in command.'

Dr John Murton, HM Ambassador to
the Democratic Republic of the Congo

'The first thing one always notices about Maud is her joy and enthusiasm. An Open Door *is a safari through a life well lived by a person who has taken the path less travelled; a woman who has lived following Christ no matter where He took her. And in every chapter she highlights the fact that God never fails.*

As one of the missionary bush pilots who flew her, I can tell you that Maud was one of our very favourite people to serve. We would arm wrestle over who would have the privilege to take trips with her and always come away encouraged and inspired to do more. To be everything she saw in us. To try to keep up with this older Irish lady who was out in front of us, being an example of what could be if we stayed close to the Lord. She was always telling us, "Oh, this is the most wonderful flight I have ever had!" Or, as we circled to land at Mulita, "Do you see all the blue tin roofs down there? You MAF pilots brought in every piece of that roofing for us." Or, "I couldn't do the things I do here if it wasn't for the part you play."

On the day we got the message Maud had been shot, we didn't know any of the circumstances surrounding the incident. The

Mulita area had been very unstable with militia causing trouble throughout the country. Information was sketchy, and we didn't know what we were flying into. But this was Maud, and every one of our pilots was ready to go for her and rushed around preparing the plane to pick her up. I had the honour of going. It always seemed like an honour to fly for this humble champion of the faith.

Maud consistently turns the focus of her story to God, giving him glory for all that was accomplished through her life. But as you read An Open Door *look in between the lines at the heart of a person who is dedicated to serving others and making her own desires match Christ's to the point that the difficult task she is assigned becomes her great joy and privilege.*

As I read, I was challenged to walk closer with the Lord, to become more like Him each day, and to finish well the work the He has given me to do. A life of significance can be a great adventure! This book reveals the secret of how to make it so.'

Jon Cadd, MAF Pilot and Program Manager East Congo

'An Open Door *is a timely and beautifully told story of a truly inspirational life. Maud's unique life journey has been filled with so many episodes of exciting and intense drama, alongside which sit endless activities dedicated to the service of the Congolese people, particularly those in the remote and isolated area of Mulita.*

This book will leave its reader amazed at what one life can accomplish, when poured out in love toward God and others in total self-sacrifice. Maud's supreme motivation is to serve the Lord Jesus Christ with all she has and to glorify His Name, whatever the cost. Unsurprisingly, God has honoured her great desire and used her life to the huge material and spiritual benefit of the people of Mulita.

These words of C. T. Studd seem an appropriate summary: "Just one life, t'will soon be past. Only what's done for Jesus will last."'

Dr Pat Morton

'Maud Kells has a quite extraordinary record of service in the cause of Christ in the Democratic Republic of the Congo. The remarkable, inspirational, and heart-warming events of her missionary life have been recorded here for the first time in book form. They bear witness to the wonderful way in which God is at work in Africa. Jean Gibson has confirmed herself as a writer of great skill in bringing to the wider church these testimonies of how Christ is being glorified in DRC. I commend this book most warmly.'

Rev. Dr Paul Bailie, Chief Executive Mission Africa

'This is not just an amazing book about Maud Kells, a woman from Cookstown working in Congo, but a power-filled story of God at work among his people.'

Pauline Kennedy, PCI Women's Ministry and Presbyterian Women Development Officer

'Maud Kells was "impelled by the voice of God to replace missionaries in Congo killed in the Simba rebellion". Simba means "lion" in Swahili and during her time in Congo, Maud was in and out of the "lion's den" many times. I have absolutely no doubt that her perseverance and ability to overcome all the difficulties she encountered in bringing the gospel and medical care to the population of Congo was, as she so vividly shares, because God was near to her and in control.

This is a compelling and riveting story which is told with great honesty. I was gripped by the fear of some moments and great rejoicing in others. Maud deliberately placed herself in situations where only God could protect her, but she knew He had guided her there. And God did protect her and provided so many instances of answered prayer that one can't deny His person or presence.

I had the privilege of doing surgical visits with Maud at Mulita and am so grateful for her example of faith, generosity and humility in the face of enormous obstacles.'

Dr Philip Wood, WEC Canada

'Maud's story is an inspiring example of life in the service of our Lord, an example that is needed in today's world. These aren't mere words on a page but a real life lived in real situations – a life lived deeply, sacrificially and faithfully for Christ. Her story inspires us to a life of faithfulness to God's calling and loving service to others. This is what will have a lasting impact in the world today.'

Susan Sutton, International Director WEC International

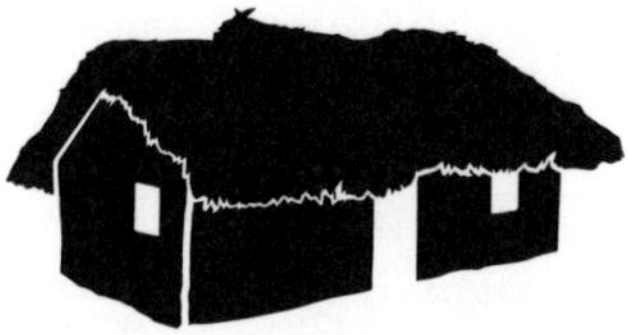

AN OPEN DOOR

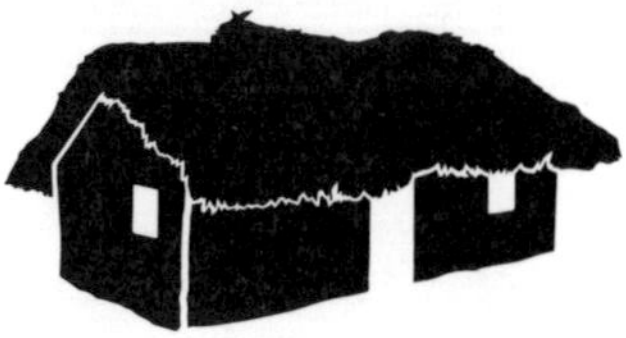

AN OPEN DOOR

A TRUE STORY OF COURAGE IN CONGO

MAUD KELLS

WITH JEAN GIBSON

10 Publishing
a division of 10 of those.com

First published in Great Britain in 2019

British Library Cataloguing in Publication Data
A record for this book is available from the British Library

ISBN: 978-1-912373-64-2

Designed and typeset by Pete Barnsley (CreativeHoot.com)
Cover image used by permission of MAF

Printed in Denmark by Nørhaven

10Publishing, a division of 10ofthose.com
Unit C, Tomlinson Road, Leyland, PR25 2DY, England

Email: info@10ofthose.com
Website: www.10ofthose.com

DEDICATION

To my Dad,

who in his ninety-eighth year continues his prayerful interest in God's work around the world.

Jean Gibson

ACKNOWLEDGEMENTS

My closest family relatives: Margaret, Dorothy, Pamela and Allan

My Molesworth church friends

My DR Congo fellow missionaries, including the pilots

My WEC International family and prayer groups

And especially the CECCA16 Church in DR Congo.

Thanks to each of you, and many others, who have prayed for and supported me over the years, so influencing my life and work for Jesus, our Precious Lord.

Maud Kells

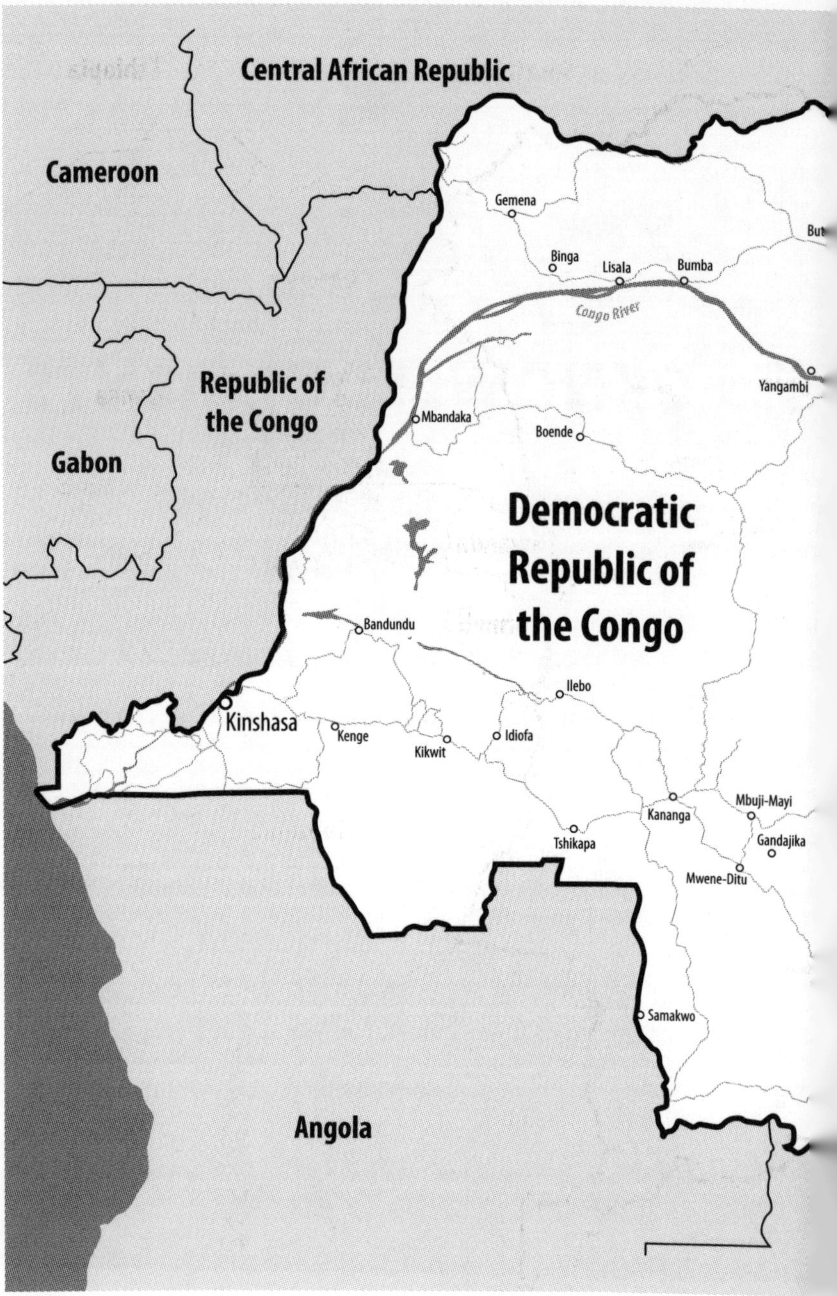

Central African Republic
Cameroon
Gemena
Binga
Lisala
Bumba
Congo River
Yangambi
Republic of the Congo
Mbandaka
Boende
Gabon
Democratic Republic of the Congo
Bandundu
Ilebo
Kinshasa
Kenge
Kikwit
Idiofa
Kananga
Mbuji-Mayi
Tshikapa
Gandajika
Mwene-Ditu
Samakwo
Angola

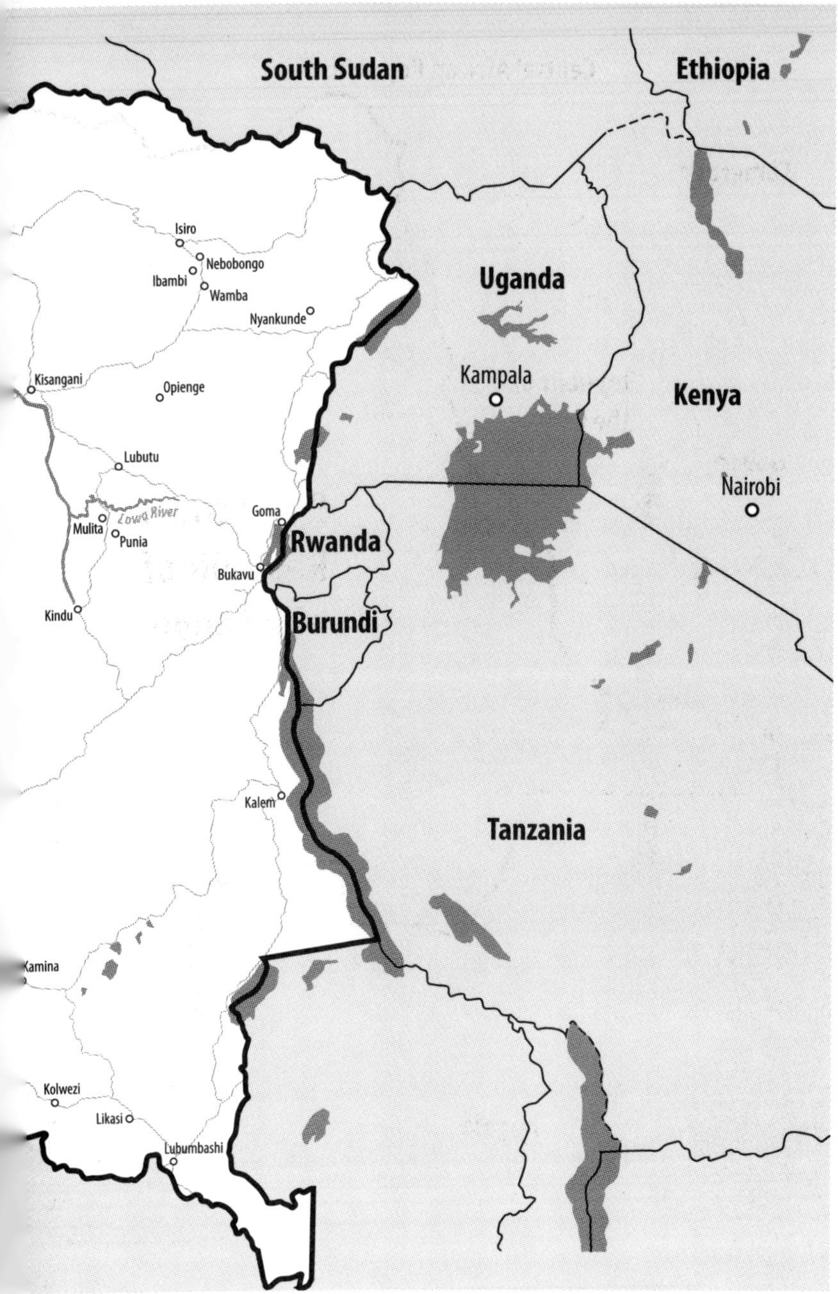

South Sudan
Ethiopia
Uganda
Kampala
Kenya
Nairobi
Isiro
Nebobongo
Ibambi
Wamba
Nyankunde
Kisangani
Opienge
Lubutu
Lowa River
Mulita
Punia
Goma
Rwanda
Bukavu
Kindu
Burundi
Kalem
Tanzania
Kamina
Kolwezi
Likasi
Lubumbashi

CONTENTS

FOREWORD

Maud tells a remarkable story – and what a story and, more, what a valiant servant of the Lord Jesus who tells the story! This is a story you need to read. I have been stirred and blessed by it.

I have known Maud since 1980 – often as she passed through our Headquarters near London as she made her many tedious journeys to and from Africa. I admired her courage. She has given so much of her life to the peoples of the Congo rain forest around the town of Mulita in one of the most isolated and poorest provinces of a chaotic country torn by violence and war.

She knew before she went that the country of her calling was dangerous – we, as a mission, had already lost missionary colleagues as martyrs just a few years before. Yet she tells her story of the years of unrest, war, evacuations and many efforts to rebuild and re-equip destroyed ministries again and again so matter-of-factly! I think she was more concerned about rats than rebels! Yet she also became a victim of the violence.

Throughout this book shines her tenacity and faith in God and her love for the people to whom God had sent her. The result has been many lives transformed physically and spiritually, and a strong church that emerged, weathering the many terrible events of the past 60 years in that area.

Maud also includes many other dedicated servants of God with whom she interacted – fellow WEC missionaries and others, the sacrificial and dangerous work of missionary pilots serving with MAF and other agencies who were her lifeline and without which Maud's ministry would have been impossible. Then there were her dear African medical and church worker colleagues who loved and supported her as she served them. Maud wanted you to see their sacrificial contributions as well.

It is no surprise that recognition has come from many – a high award in Congo – the first foreigner to be so honoured, an OBE in the UK, and the Inspirational Woman of the Year Award in Northern Ireland.

May her story indeed inspire many to similar commitment to serve God and humankind!

Patrick Johnstone
Author Emeritus, ***Operation World***
WEC International

INTRODUCTION

Over the years as I have recounted my stories, many people have asked if I have written a book to share these accounts of God's deliverance and undertaking. I have always answered, 'No', because I want God alone to receive the glory for all that I have experienced and accomplished in my life.

'But you can give Him the glory if you write them down,' I was told.

Hence the reason for this book: to give glory to our wonderful Lord Jesus. As I quote in it, 'Let the one who boasts boast in the Lord' (1 Corinthians 1:31).

Only He and His Promises have carried me through the many difficult circumstances in my life. The Living Bible paraphrase of 2 Corinthians 12:9, 'I am with you; that is all you need', has been His word to me many times when I was at my wits' end in Africa and Northern Ireland.

In the course of time a few authors offered to write my story, but finally the Lord confirmed to me that Jean

Gibson should be the one to write it down. I am very grateful for all the hard work she has put into deciphering my prayer letters and interviews to record them in this book.

Again, though, I would like to reiterate the one big purpose in writing this book: to glorify my wonderful Lord and Saviour Jesus Christ.

Maud Kells

1

THE ATTACK

The African night was quiet as I closed the shutters and prepared for bed. A whiff of smoke from dying fires hung in the air. It had been the usual busy Sunday and I was still recovering from the New Year celebrations on Thursday with all the attendant distribution of food and clothes. Onande, my night guard, moved around outside, checking the compound, making sure the gates were well secured with ropes. On occasion his system worked so well the midwife from the hospital was unable to undo them if she needed me in the night, forcing her to waken me by shouting over the hedge. Tonight, however, there was no shouting. My neighbours were already settled for the night and only the high-pitched chirp of crickets and the occasional croak of a nearby frog disturbed the silence.

'*Mademoiselle*, are you awake?' I fought my way into consciousness and checked the time as the knocking on the shutters woke me. Just after midnight. I had had a couple of hours' sleep. I recognised Mama Rebecca's voice.

'What's the problem?'

'A mama has come to maternity who has had three caesarean sections before.'

I blinked the sleep out of my eyes as I assessed the situation. 'How is she? How is the baby's heartbeat?'

'Everything is fine. She is not in any danger. I'm just letting you know.'

I was pleased that Rebecca the midwife had heeded my request to be kept informed of emergencies but it sounded as though all was under control. 'Do you need me for anything? Is there a nurse surgeon there to do a caesarean section?'

'We are fine, we can cope. Nguza and Ramazone are there. I just wanted to let you know what was happening.'

'Very good. If there are any problems, if you need IVs or medical supplies from the house here, come back and call me.'

'That's fine. I'll do that.'

I settled back into bed, grateful for trained staff who ensured I no longer needed to deal personally with each situation.

'*Madame*, please come, it's an emergency. No one else can do it. We need you.'

I shot awake again. It was a male voice this time. Only fifteen minutes had passed since the previous call. The knocking on the shutters was insistent.

'I've talked to the midwife, I've dealt with that problem.

Everything is under control.' I tried to sound patient. It was probably an overanxious husband in a panic.

'No, no. You need to come immediately. The lady's very ill. They have sent me to get you.'

'Why? She's having a caesarean section, she'll be okay,' I tried to reassure him.

'No, no. You need to come.'

With a sigh, I dressed quickly and slipped my feet into my sandals. Although my bedroom was beside the front door, the key for the Yale lock on that door had been lost during the war so I went out through the back door, locking it behind me. Onande met me on the doorstep.

'*Mademoiselle*, I heard you talking to someone. Do you need to go to the hospital?'

'Yes, I think it's the husband of a maternity patient who is insisting that I go.'

'I'm coming with you.' The hospital compound was only 300 yards from mine but Onande took his protective duties seriously. We checked that the back door was securely locked and set off together, the white dust path picked out in the light of my torch. The gate of my compound was already open and I wondered vaguely whether Rebecca had left it open, or the husband who had come to my window.

Between the maternity department and the operating suite, a group of people had gathered: hospital staff and relatives of the patient.

'*Mademoiselle*, why have you come?' One of the midwives was confused.

'The man said you needed me. Didn't you send him to call me?'

'No, we didn't send anyone.'

'Where is the husband of the patient? I'm sure he was the one who called me.'

'I think he's in the theatre with his wife, in the waiting area.'

'Well, I don't understand it. Do you need me for anything?'

'No, no. Everything is under control.'

I looked at Onande. All appeared calm. 'Then we'll just go back.'

I was aware of a slight unease. In all my years at the hospital I had never had a hoax call. We went back through the gate of the compound and up the side of the house towards the back door. Suddenly out of the darkness ran two masked figures in camouflage clothing pointing something shaped like a gun, covered in leaves. One of them grabbed Onande and ran off with him. For a moment I froze, then thought of the cash I kept in the house in the absence of local banks. Doubtless a seventy-five-year-old lady seemed an easy target.

'You won't scare me; you won't get the better of me,' flashed through my mind as I reached out to grab the weapon. The noise and the pain were instantaneous. I didn't realise a gunshot would be so loud. Pain shot through me from front to back. A scream that seemed to come from somewhere else brought my attacker up short and he took to his heels as I continued to yell at the top of my voice. It was my only means of getting help but a disturbing stillness followed my screams. Where were the neighbours, the pastor, the *chef de poste*, the hospital staff?[1]

Blood was pouring from a wound between my shoulders where the bullet appeared to have passed through. Desperate to stem the bleeding, I staggered to the wall of the house, pressing myself against it as firmly as possible. Time seemed to stretch indefinitely as I stood there, fighting to stay conscious and keep the blood flow under control. Call after call elicited no response. Images flitted through my brain: pictures of Jesus left on the cross, crucified and alone. As on that night, people were too terrified to come near and identify with the victim. It looked as if this was it. I would die here in Mulita where I had invested so much over the years.

I had no fear. I was very conscious of God's presence surrounding me and the Holy Spirit's whisper that He was in complete control of the whole situation. He reminded me of Scriptures that had been precious over the years: 'The Lord will keep your going out and your coming in' (Psalm 121:8, ESV); 'My help comes from the Lord, who made heaven and earth' (Psalm 121:2, ESV). While I was standing there with no physical help appearing, I thought, 'Lord, are you taking me now?' I prayed my daily prayer whatever the situation: 'Forgive me, Lord, for anything I've done wrong.' Then I added, 'I'm ready to go, Lord. But there are a few things I'd like to finish off on earth before I go.'

'*Mademoiselle* is dying! *Mademoiselle* is dying!' A Congolese friend, Mado, visiting me in Mulita, appeared from the guest house where she was staying. Having suffered from hearing problems all her life, it was ironic that she should be the first to respond to my screams. As she joined in my attempt to call for help, Mado shouted, '*Mademoiselle* is dead! *Mademoiselle* is dead!'

'*Mademoiselle* is manifestly not dead,' I thought to myself. '*Mademoiselle* is still shouting!'

Onande, a wiry little man, having managed to wriggle free and escape the bandits, came running up, taking in the situation as he tried to get his breath back. 'I'll go to the pastor's house and call him.' Realising the pastor was too frightened to come out of his house, Onande dashed off to reassure him that the bandits had gone. His explanation seemed to have the desired effect because almost immediately I heard the drum going as an emergency message went out to the community.

I was frozen to the wall, keeping pressure on my back as firm as possible. I could still feel the blood dribbling from my wound and knew that once I moved it would be difficult to stop.

However I could not stand there indefinitely. As the medical staff supported me into the house, shock and blood loss took over and everything grew dim as I collapsed onto a mat on the floor.

2

THE CALL

My entry into the world was a foretaste of dramas to come. My older sister had been born in a nursing home in Belfast without any difficulty, so my mother decided she would have her second child at home on their farm near Cookstown and avoid the eighty-kilometre journey to the city. As the night progressed, however, the doctor struggled to do a difficult forceps delivery. The battered and bruised child who appeared in the morning seemed reluctant to face such a hostile world. By the next evening my father, convinced I was dying, went again for the doctor.

The disgruntled physician offered little hope. 'Willie Andrew, there is no way that I am going to lose another night's sleep over that baby. She couldn't possibly survive after all I had to do last night to haul her into the world. Nurse McKay will help you to care for her but it will be a miracle if she survives.'

Obstinate from the beginning, I refused to die. My parents watched as I clung to life, gathering strength by the day and proving everyone wrong.

I was an April Fool's baby, born on 1 April 1939. Six months after I was born, Neville Chamberlain announced on the radio that Britain was at war with Germany. I was of course unaware of the momentous happenings on the world stage during my first six years, although I do remember English soldiers coming to our farm and calling me 'wee blondie'. As part of the United Kingdom, Northern Ireland was automatically involved in the war, bringing blackout blinds to our windows and ration books to buy sweets and groceries.

I lived in a divided country. Since 1922, the island of Ireland had been divided into two separate jurisdictions: twenty-six counties in the southern part becoming the Irish Free State and the remaining six counties in the north opting to remain in the United Kingdom. The six counties were known as Northern Ireland or Ulster while the Irish Free State became known as Eire, the Irish form of Ireland. In 1948 the Republic of Ireland Act stated that the twenty-six counties of Ireland previously known as the Irish Free State could be officially described as the Republic of Ireland. Little did I realise that being born in one land that changed its name over the years, I would end up living in another with a similar need to portray its identity with a changing name.

Despite my difficult beginning, I thrived well on our home-farm produce. I came down the stairs each morning to the smell of bacon frying in the pan as my mother cooked breakfast on the Modern Mistress cast-iron stove. The farm dogs, a fox terrier and a collie, lay under the Modern Mistress in the evenings, having spent the day outdoors with my father. Like all country houses around us at the time, and indeed our little country school, we had no electricity or running water. Toilets were outside and were dug-out pit latrines. We carried water from the well or pump. The kitchen stove was our main source of heat, except for Christmas when an open turf fire burned in the sitting room. The smell of burning turf would always evoke for me the atmosphere of Christmas.

My sister Margaret and I were joined by two younger sisters, Irene and Dorothy. The farm was our playground and the cows coming in to be milked each morning and evening formed a secure framework to our day. In the summer holidays we played in the laurel and rhododendron bushes, or in the larger beech trees behind our house, and rode on the hay cart drawn by our majestic Cheshire horse. A highlight of the summer holidays was the week spent in Portstewart on the north coast, learning to swim, eating ice cream in Morelli's cafe, and sometimes attending CSSM (Children's Special Service Mission) meetings on the steps near the paddling pools.

On the farm, the hay barn was one of our favourite places, where we could climb and hide in the hay and straw. My father's threshing machine, stored in the barn, offered many opportunities for imaginative games. One day, playing at the base of the shaft where the chaff came out, I put my hand down on a squirming nest of baby rats. 'Uggh!' I screeched, snatching my hand away. 'Look what I touched!' I recoiled in revulsion at the feel of those wriggling bodies. The terror generated by that experience would remain with me for years to come.

While my parents knew nothing of a personal relationship with God, their Scottish Presbyterian background dictated a strict Saturday night pattern. Everyone polished their shoes, had their weekly turn in the tin bath in front of the kitchen stove and washed their hair. Sometimes my long blonde hair was put into ringlets, using rolled up paper, ready for Sunday school and church the next day. Potatoes and vegetables were peeled and as much preparation as possible made for Sunday, which was honoured as the Sabbath day, a day of rest.

As a family we were members of Molesworth Presbyterian Church in Cookstown. The railway line running past our house provided a convenient shortcut which we took each Sunday as children, risking our lives as we made our way to Sunday school. We perfected the technique of feeling the vibration of a train coming up the line so that we could get off the railway track before it reached us.

Our spiritual instruction did not prevent us stealing delicious little pears on our way home from church each Sunday in the autumn season. The pear tree was situated on the edge of our neighbour's farmyard which we ran through as quickly as possible. We were not afraid of being caught stealing pears but of being attacked by the ganders which objected to our intrusion and flew at us.

After church the family came home to a traditional Sunday dinner of roast beef, vegetables and potatoes, which our live-in maid ate with us as part of the family. Dessert was usually oven-cooked rice made with milk, accompanied by stewed apples or rhubarb from the garden. In the afternoon, while my father slept, my mother walked with us to our grandmother's house about three kilometres away, where we enjoyed meeting up with our cousins.

Some incidents stand out in my memory. One afternoon, when no one was about, I stood on an old potato box at the half door of an outhouse and addressed the empty farmyard, regarded only by the dogs and a few hens. For some reason I recited to them the twenty-third psalm. That experience stayed with me, as if God was speaking to me in some way.

On another occasion, when I was a young teenager, the local station master came to take the Bible class before church, filling in for a teacher who was unable to be there. A squat figure, with his head to one side, he explained that he was 'born again'.

'We all need to be saved,' he said. 'Just as Paul preached to the people in the book of Acts, "Believe on the Lord Jesus and you shall be saved."' Although I did not fully understand what he meant, something about that talk stood out for me.

I struggled to do well at Cookstown high school but from an early age I wanted to be a nurse. The aunt after whom I was called had trained as a nurse in the Royal Victoria Hospital in Belfast. As she and her husband lived nearby, we saw them often and a special bond developed between Aunt Maude and myself. Influenced and inspired by her, I wanted to follow in her footsteps.

I was a quiet child, nervous and apprehensive about meeting new people. If I was going to be a nurse, I decided it would be easier to do children's nursing than relate to adults. When I was accepted onto the course in the Royal Belfast Hospital for Sick Children, Aunt Maude took me into the sitting room of her house for a private talk. We sat down together on the sofa and Aunt Maude looked me in the eye.

'You'll be going to Belfast soon, Maud,' she said. 'I've done nursing training and I know what it's like. It will be hard at times and some people won't stick at it, but make sure you don't give up easily. It will be worth it in the end. Keep persevering with your training, no matter what difficulties and problems you encounter.'

'I understand, Aunt Maude.' I arranged the folds of my skirt and tried to still the fluttering in my stomach at the thought of what lay ahead. 'I'll remember what you said. I won't give up, no matter what happens.'

She reached out to pat my knee. 'I know you'll do your best. Just think about what I've said when you're having a hard day. Remember we'll be praying for you.'

I followed Aunt Maude out of the room and as we joined the others I vowed in my heart not to let her down.

Her advice would stay with me, throughout my training and long afterwards.

On 8 April 1957, my mother's birthday, I travelled to Belfast on the bus with my mother. An austere sister tutor met us, cast her eye over me and said, 'Say goodbye to your mother and come with me.' As she turned on her heel, I had no option but to follow.

As Aunt Maude had predicted, the training was tough and some who started with me did not finish. Some of the sisters on the wards were demanding and difficult to work with; one sister tutor in particular terrified me. However I made up my mind I was going to work hard and do my best. I wanted to excel at nursing so I entered my training with that goal in mind.

Sitting alone one evening in the nurses' sitting room, I was approached by a nurse who had spotted this quiet newcomer in the corner. 'Hello, I'm Trudy Ussher. Have you just started? Come and meet the others.'

She shepherded me across the room to where a group was chatting together. 'This is Maud. She's just come from Cookstown.'

Her friends looked round with a smile, apparently happy to have me intruding on their conversation. 'Hello, Maud, come and join us. Here's a seat. I'm Mary McCandless.'

The girls were happy and friendly in a way I had not experienced before. I soon realised that they called themselves Christians and when they invited me to the Nurses Christian Fellowship on Tuesday evenings, I was happy to attend. It was reassuring to have friends and somewhere to go together.

There was something about these girls that attracted me to the Christian faith. Having attended church and Sunday school throughout my childhood, I knew about God. However as I spent time with these nurses, I realised I was not what they called a Christian. I had no understanding of how I could have a relationship with God as they described it.

I had the idea that some people became emotionally worked up at meetings and had some sort of crisis which they called being 'saved' or 'born again'. As I came to know my new friends, however, I became more curious about what the term 'Christian' meant. I began questioning the meaning of life: why was I here? What if there really was a heaven and hell? I tried reading my Bible but it was difficult to understand. I prayed that if God was real, He would reveal Himself to me.

One evening I was visiting my aunt Maude and her husband, who was now retired from the Presbyterian ministry. At the end of the evening, as he was leaving me at the bus stop, he challenged me about my relationship with God. 'You know,' he said, 'the most important thing you can do in life is to invite God to be in control of it.'

Just as the bus was coming, a verse of Scripture I had heard many times came to me: 'Behold, I stand at the door and knock. If anyone hears my voice and opens the door, I will come in to him and eat with him, and he with me' (Revelation 3:20, ESV). At that bus stop in Derriaghy, that is exactly what I did. I asked God to forgive me and to come into my life. And my life changed there. On the journey back to the Nurses Home, I felt God's presence with me in a real way for the first time. In that moment I did not understand all that following Christ meant, but I had a desire to serve and follow Him. It set everything that happened afterwards in a different context.

In the following days, as I wondered what my future held as a Christian, I came across Isaiah 41:10 in my Bible:

> *So do not fear, for I am with you;*
> *do not be dismayed, for I am your God.*
> *I will strengthen you and help you;*
> *I will uphold you with my righteous right hand.*

That promise was the first of many promises God would give me, but it would stay with me throughout the years to come. It kept me strong as I completed my children's training and moved to the nearby Royal Victoria Hospital to do my general training over the next two and a half years.

Although nursing was demanding, it had its lighter moments. One night I heard the lift coming up to the neurology ward where I was working and went to investigate, presuming an emergency patient was being admitted. The lift doors opened to reveal a trolley which appeared to be carrying a dead body. The only nurse on the ward that night, I was somewhat taken aback when the trolley propelled itself out of the lift towards me. Recovering from my initial shock, I realised someone was playing a prank and decided to get my own back. Stepping into the kitchen, I filled a pot with water and threw it over the corpse, achieving the quickest and most dramatic resurrection ever seen. The nurse propelling the trolley from underneath and the corpse on top both disappeared, leaving a trail of water in their wake.

During my training several things helped me grow as a young Christian. On Sundays I went with my friends to a local church. Any of us who were free on a Saturday evening would go to the Rendezvous gatherings in the Wellington Hall in Belfast, where we enjoyed meeting with other young Christians and benefitted from teaching and worship together. My Christian friends had also talked to me about the importance of reading Scripture and I was amazed as that began to mean something to me. I found that Scripture Union notes helped me understand what I was reading and my daily 'quiet time' became very precious.

One day Mary and Trudy came to me: 'Some of us have been invited to speak at a meeting on Sunday evening. Would you like to come with us and share how you came to know God personally?'

The idea of speaking in public was almost too much for me to contemplate; I found it difficult to talk to anyone about anything, never mind speak publicly about something so personal. 'I've never done anything like that before. I don't know if I could do it,' I protested.

The idea terrified me but my friends encouraged me to try: 'We're all nervous but it is good for us to share our faith. God helps us to find the right words.'

With great misgivings I agreed. The following Sunday I accompanied Mary and Trudy to a little mission hall in Belfast where around thirty people had gathered. A man at the door greeted us with enthusiasm and showed us into the front row, where I sat immobilised by fear. Somehow at the appropriate point I managed to tell my story, with much prayer that God would help me and not let me run out of words in the middle.

Though nervous and stumbling that first time I spoke in public, the next time was easier. I came to realise that daunting as they were, these opportunities were strengthening my faith. The congregations were sometimes small but they seemed to appreciate our efforts and we learned to rely on the power of God's Holy Spirit to help us communicate what He wanted us to say.

A highlight each year was the Worldwide Missionary Convention in Bangor, County Down. This had been started in 1937 by Herbie Mateer. He brought missionary speakers from around the world, giving us first-hand information on God's work worldwide and raising large sums of money for missions. An interest in spreading the gospel overseas began in my heart as I sat in those meetings, seeking God's will for my life and wanting to serve Him with all that I was, whatever that would mean.

As I learned to hear the Lord speaking to me, I began to underline all the occurrences of 'fear not' and 'be strong and of a good courage' in my Bible. Those promises became very significant to my naturally nervous disposition. If God was going to look after me, then why should I fear or give up? I really wanted to follow Him but had no idea what it might mean. I would have to trust Him to fulfil these promises.

As Mary and I moved to Edinburgh to do midwifery training, my prayer was that God would show me His plan for my life. In answer God brought into my life two special people. Flo Green and Alice Harris were ladies in their sixties to whom God had given a ministry to nurses in Edinburgh. Their home, Rehoboth ('open spaces'), was kept as an open house for nurses which we used on our days off or even for a couple of hours between shifts. There we relaxed in the spiritual oasis which these ladies had created as a facility for young nurses away from home. As I thought about the way forward, Flo and Alice prayed and encouraged me to serve God with my whole heart.

I was beginning to feel that perhaps God wanted me to go overseas as a missionary but how could I be sure? I was aware of other women who had followed the call of God overseas. At the time international attention was focused on women such as the WEC missionary Dr Helen Roseveare, who had been held by Congo rebels for five months and was still recovering from the traumas of that experience.

I was conscious of my own inadequacies. These other women were strong and courageous. I could never do anything like that. Yet I could not get the idea out of my mind.

One day I decided to skip dinner so that I could fast and pray, asking God for a sign. I went up to my bedroom, closed the door, got down on my knees and asked God to show me if He wanted me to be a missionary. As I opened the Scripture Union notes for the day, Revelation 3:8 jumped out at me: 'See, I have placed before you an open door that no one can shut. I know that you have little strength, yet you have kept my word and have not denied my name.'

I felt God speaking directly to me. He knew all about my feelings of inadequacy but He understood that I wanted to follow Him above all. He was placing an open door before me.

Yet at the back of my mind persisted another voice: 'Perhaps you're just reading what you want to hear into this Scripture; God's not really calling you at all.' As I wrestled with these thoughts, I prayed that if He was really calling me, then within twenty-four hours I would hear something about a Bible school. I was 'putting out a fleece' like Gideon in the Old Testament.

The next day when I came off duty I went to my pigeon hole as usual to look for letters. I found an envelope containing information about the Bible Training Institute in Glasgow with no indication where it had come from. I knew God was saying to me, 'Now do you believe me? I'm calling you into full-time work.' I had a concrete sign with which I could not argue. Soon afterwards Flo gave me a leaflet about the Worldwide

Evangelisation Crusade (WEC). As I prayed, I knew that God was calling me to this mission.

It was 1964. I was twenty-five years old and had no idea what lay ahead.

3

THE OPEN DOOR

As I finished my midwifery training in Edinburgh in December 1964, I found a vacancy waiting for me in the WEC Missionary Training College in Glasgow, known as MTC. Before making the transition, however, there was one remaining hurdle to overcome – I had to let my parents know my decision.

We were sitting around the kitchen table, enjoying my mother's Sunday roast, when my father broached the subject. 'Have you applied for any jobs? Are you planning to come back to Northern Ireland?'

I swallowed and took a deep breath. The smell of roast beef added to the churning of my stomach. I forced the words out. 'I'm not going to be a nurse in the UK.' I toyed with my food. 'God has called me to the mission field overseas. I don't know where it will be yet, but I have a place in the WEC Missionary Training College in Glasgow for the next two years.'

The news dropped like a bombshell in the middle of the dinner table. My father set down his knife and fork and looked at me. He had no understanding of the words 'God has called me'. 'Why would you do that after all your hard work, getting through all your training? Are you going to throw away all that you've achieved to waste your life as a missionary?' His voice rose in disbelief.

'I'm sorry, I hate to go against your wishes. But I have to follow God's call.'

Shocked, my mother internalised her concerns and said very little, quietly supportive of whatever I wanted to do. I left the dinner table feeling torn. I wanted to honour my parents, yet God's call on my life was higher than their reservations and I knew I had to follow where He was leading.

I arrived at MTC, a new student once again. Excited to explore what God had in store for me, I faced the next phase with a mixture of anticipation and fear, but also a huge sense of relief in knowing God's plan for my life. I was determined to benefit as much as possible from the training offered by WEC.

When I worried about my ability to do what God was asking of me, I turned to the verses He had given me from 1 Corinthians 1:27–29: 'But God chose the foolish things of the world to shame the wise; God chose the weak things of the world to shame the strong. God chose the lowly things of this world and the despised things – and the things that are not – to nullify the things that are, so that no one may boast before him.' I held onto these words. I might feel inadequate but God had chosen me. He would equip me for the task ahead.

Of course it meant that I had to start studying again. We began with the whole fascinating history of WEC and its founder, Charles Thomas Studd, usually known as C.T. Studd. Born in England in 1860, he turned his back on his privileged upbringing to follow God's call overseas. After twenty-one years, having served in China with Hudson Taylor and then in India, C.T. Studd returned to England in poor health. One night he saw a meeting advertised with the words 'Cannibals need Christ'. Intrigued, he went in, and was challenged by the need of people in the heart of Africa who had never had the opportunity to hear about Christ. Leaving behind family and friends, with no organisation to support him, C.T. Studd sailed alone for Africa in 1910. People told him he was crazy to contemplate such a task. His reply has echoed down the years: 'If Jesus Christ be God and died for me, then no sacrifice can be too great for me to make for Him.'

In 1913 he set off again with Alfred Buxton, through Kenya and Uganda, to north-eastern Congo. There he started the Heart of Africa Mission. His wife, Priscilla, at home with their four daughters, set up the mission's UK headquarters in the same year. Aware of God's call not just to Africa but to the whole unevangelised world, C.T. Studd renamed his mission the Worldwide Evangelisation Crusade, now known as WEC International.

Reading about C.T. Studd and other missionary pioneers inspired me to make God's will my single focus.

As I prayed about it and asked God where He wanted me to serve Him, a great longing developed in my heart to work in a place like Congo, where few had heard the gospel. What a privilege it would be to take Christ's name to those who had never heard of Him. The excitement of such a thought thrilled me, and yet I wanted to be sure that it was what God wanted me to do, not just some romantic idea on my part.

When I came home to Ireland for the Easter holidays in 1965, a memorial service was planned in the Wellington Hall, Belfast for missionaries who had died in Congo the previous year. The country had achieved independence from Belgium in June 1960 and was now known as the Republic of the Congo. For five years since then, political upheaval and conflict had torn the country apart and had become known as the Congo Crisis. In 1964 the Simba rebellion had broken out. The staff of Nebobongo hospital, including Dr Helen Roseveare, had suffered humiliating abuse during a time of captivity. A story unfolded of beatings, torture, rape and murder. Five WEC missionaries were among those who died.

At the memorial service my friend and I made our way up into the balcony of the Wellington Hall, where we looked out over the crowd below. The date was 1 April, my birthday. One of the Bible readings was from Revelation 7, the passage of Scripture God had used to speak to me that very morning, describing a great multitude from every nation standing before the throne of God. I knew the Lord was challenging me through those verses; He was reiterating the call He had placed on my life the year before. At the end of the service there was an appeal for young people willing to go to replace those who had been martyred. Everything within me responded as I felt God's challenge to my heart. I knew with a deep certainty that He wanted me to go to Congo.

The context of that call to Congo was suffering, as we remembered those who had given everything. With my timid nature, going into the dangers of Congo was the antithesis of what I would naturally have chosen to do. Yet somehow the voice of God's Spirit in my heart lifted me beyond my fears. I was called to take up the cross and follow; He would look after everything else.

When I returned to college after the holidays, I had a meeting with the committee helping to guide students as they looked to the future. I looked round at Frank and Elsie Rowbothom, founders of the training college, Bill Chapman, the principal, and a number of others. 'I know what I'm going to do now,' I exclaimed with a smile. 'God has called me to Congo.'

Silence fell. In the wake of the Congo crisis and the happenings of the previous year, I should have guessed what their response might be: 'The door to Congo is closed. Pray about it and ask God to show you another country. Congo is out of the question.'

I was confused. On the one hand I believed God had put our leaders in place to guide us, yet on the other He had clearly said He had set before me an open door and given me the promise from Revelation 3:8 that no one could shut it. Over the following months I kept seeking His will and tried to keep an open mind, but He did not show me any other place to go. I knew that if He wanted me in Congo, He would open the way for me, so I continued my training and kept the dream alive in my heart – even though others questioned my leading.

WEC was a faith-based fellowship and did not pay salaries. Anyone wishing to go overseas with them needed to be prepared to live by faith that God would provide for their needs in the years ahead. To me this was not an issue. If God had gone to such lengths to confirm His plan for my life, He would provide for me in the place to which He was leading me.

While I was at MTC, the Lord taught me many lessons about living by faith. One morning I read Matthew 10:29: 'Are not two sparrows sold for a penny? Yet not one of them shall fall to the ground outside your Father's care ... So don't be afraid; you are worth more than many sparrows.' I went out for a prayer walk before breakfast and on the footpath in front of me spotted a little dead sparrow. I could hardly believe my eyes; God was demonstrating His Fatherly love and care in a visible form.

I spent the summer of 1966 working with Operation Mobilisation in France, trying to refresh my very basic, schoolgirl French in preparation for going to French-speaking Congo. As was the custom in OM, I put all my money into 'the pool' from which our needs were supplied.

Travelling back home before the rest of the team in order to be bridesmaid at my sister Irene's wedding, I worked out the least expensive route to Northern Ireland. This entailed a train to Calais, ferry to Dover and train to Heathrow Airport in London for a standby midnight flight back to Belfast. I only had enough money for that flight, with not even enough left over for a cup of coffee.

When I arrived at the check-in desk, about 9 p.m., a number of people were already on the standby waiting list for the flight I wanted. 'I'm sorry. There's no possibility of getting a seat tonight. The list is too long.' The desk attendant was polite but firm.

'I have to get on that flight. Please add my name to the list anyway, even if it is long.' I was equally firm.

I returned to the waiting area to pray that God would overrule. I turned to my Bible reading for the day, Matthew 6:25–34: '... do not worry about your life ... Look at the birds of the air ... Are you not much more valuable than they? ... But seek first his kingdom and his righteousness, and all these things will be given to you as well.'

Three hours later, when the booked passengers had been called to board the plane, I returned to the check-in desk to overhear the pilot speaking to the attendant. 'Are there any standby passengers?'

'Yes, lots. There's a long list.'

'Well, I can take five.'

The attendant read out five names, with mine fifth on the list. Pushing my luggage forward to be weighed, I heard her say, 'There's no time to weigh luggage. Just take it and run.' Gathering up my overweight camping gear, I scampered on to the flight with a prayer of thankfulness for God's provision.

On arrival in Belfast my mother and a good friend, Sally Moffett, were waiting to take me home. Sally handed me an envelope from her brother, Jim, and I opened it to find a substantial sum of money. My heart was full of joy, not just because I had received money to cover the fees for my final term of college, but because I understood what it meant to 'seek first his kingdom and his righteousness' and find all the other things added to it.

I finished my two years' missionary training in Glasgow, followed by six months at the candidates' course in the WEC headquarters in London. Still holding onto my call to Congo, I needed to go next to Belgium to do a tropical diseases course and study French. It was my first extended time outside the United Kingdom. Apprehension of the unknown was greater than my excitement at living overseas. My fearful nature must have made me one of the most unlikely candidates for a war-torn country like Congo when the prospect of going for a long period to Europe generated sleepless nights. I arrived in Brussels, where most people spoke French; I had five months to learn how to communicate with them.

Managing to achieve the language diploma I needed, I moved to Antwerp in the month of March to tackle a four-month tropical diseases course. With the inhabitants of Antwerp speaking Flemish, I was thrown into a different language situation, and sometimes had little idea of what was happening around me. Yet the tropical diseases course was in French, in which we were expected to be fluent enough to follow the somewhat technical vocabulary.

One consolation was that I did not have to tackle this alone. In Antwerp I discovered that Rhoda Gill, a Scottish girl with whom I had done midwifery training in Edinburgh, was doing the same course. Not only was she studying with me but she had the same goal in view – she was planning to go to Congo, though with a different mission, the Regions Beyond Missionary Union. In the midst of so many experiences that were unfamiliar, I was delighted to have a friend.

Unfortunately two unpleasant guests appeared in our accommodation. The fear of mice, which had plagued me since my childhood, surfaced again. My mother, concerned about whether I was eating enough in this foreign country, sent me parcels of food and cakes. One day I opened the wardrobe in my room to discover my mother's cake stored there had been sampled by a four-footed visitor. The thought of these creatures sharing my bedroom made me shudder. It was enough to put me off my sleep and drive thoughts of study from my mind.

Together Rhoda and I managed to find a trap and get rid of them. However the thought of the mice remained with me, haunting my dreams. I prayed and trusted the Lord to deliver me from this terrible fear, knowing that in Congo they had not only mice but rats. If God wanted me to survive in Congo, He would somehow have to help me deal with this phobia.

In 1968 I completed the courses in Belgium and by that time the door to Congo was open again. Although unrest was still widespread in the country, some of the more experienced missionaries, including Helen Roseveare, had returned from 1966 onwards, testing out the situation. Following their reports, WEC felt they could now send new missionaries to fill the gaps left by those who had died. God was fulfilling the promise He had given me, confirming again where He wanted me to go.

At that time WEC had a wonderful lady called Olga Hamlett who produced lists of essential items for all new missionaries preparing to go overseas. Armed with my list, I headed off to the Army and Navy stores for mosquito nets, a Primus stove, a camp bed and other basics I would need to survive in Congo. Olga looked after all the practical details for us, obtaining tickets and visas and advising us on all that needed to be done. Despite appearing old-fashioned to us young missionaries, this caring and efficient lady made it much easier for us as we prepared to travel.

On 4 October, the evening before I left home, I read the story of Jacob going to Egypt and realised that, like me, he was holding onto God to see him through the unknown way ahead. As I prepared to set off for Congo, God's words to Jacob came to me in a very personal way: 'I will go down to Egypt with you, and I will surely bring you back again' (Genesis 46:4). It was one of the promises that I noted then and would turn to in times of uncertainty in the days to come.

The next day I left home to go to WEC headquarters in Bulstrode, feeling a tug at leaving my parents who did not fully understand my decision. It was particularly difficult to say goodbye to my father who was convinced he would never see me again. Yet I was aware of God helping me keep my composure during those farewell moments and I left trusting in all the promises God was giving me. Willie Weir, the WEC representative in Ireland, saw me off in Belfast, along with his wife, Beth, and other friends. In my diary I wrote, 'Hallelujah! Off to Congo!'

A good night's sleep on the ferry from Belfast to Heysham set me up for the long train journey to Bulstrode the next day. There I met Isobel Laverick from Newcastle in England, also bound for Congo with WEC. That night the WEC family in Bulstrode commissioned us with a special time of worship and prayer.

On the morning of 7 October Jean Walker and Nancy Lindsay, two Irish WEC missionaries, took Isobel and myself to Victoria train station, where we met up with Rhoda, my friend from Belgium. On 10 October 1968 we sailed out of Antwerp on the *Lumumba*, named after the first president of the newly independent Congo.

The journey through the Bay of Biscay was predictably rough and our excitement dimmed in the throes of seasickness. Isobel and I spent much of our time reading in our bunks, doped with sea sickness pills. I read the story of Winnie Davies, a missionary nurse who had died in Congo during the Simba rebellion, and was inspired by her commitment to stay with the people to whom God had called her. Throughout the journey I constantly reminded myself of the promises God had given me. My Bible and the devotional book *Streams in the Desert* were very precious during this time of travel and inner preparation.

I found the ship a great novelty, never having seen anything like it before; it seemed such a waste to be ill that first week, rather than being able to enter into all that it offered. More seasoned travellers were enjoying the swimming pool, tennis courts and other activities. Eventually I managed to emerge from my bunk but it was some time before I recovered enough to do justice to the variety of food on offer at mealtime.

After the first week we stopped at the Canary Islands to refuel; it was a relief after all the sickness to be on dry land for a few hours. The second week on the ship was calmer and much more enjoyable, allowing us to sample the swimming pool and sunbathe on deck. As we crossed the equator, we appreciated the clouds that shielded us from the worst of the heat and the breeze on deck that reduced the temperatures. I was luxuriating in something of a bubble, removed from the realities of life at home behind me and life in Congo ahead of me.

On 24 October 1968 I woke at daybreak to discover we were making our way up the Congo River. As I looked out across that expanse of water on the morning of our arrival, I felt a thrill; I thought, 'I must capture this, I must hold this image in my memory. This is my first view of Congo.' The wide estuary lined with palm trees glittered in the sunshine; on each side the forest stretched into the distance. There was no one in sight, just the blue African sky reflected in the water that led to an unknown future. As we made our dignified progress into the port of Matadi, I thought, 'This is it. I've arrived.'

4

FIRST IMPRESSIONS

The euphoria of disembarking from the *Lumumba* and stepping on to Congolese soil for the first time evaporated in the African sunshine.

'Can I take your passport please?' A man held out his hand for our documents.

Conscious of my vulnerability in this new unknown, all I could think of was the instruction we had been given before leaving home: 'Don't let anyone take your passport out of your hand. Ever.' Alarm swept through me.

'We were warned not to let anyone take our passports.' I clutched it in a panic.

The Swedish missionary who had come to help us through immigration and customs was somewhat nonplussed by my reluctance to trust him. As there appeared to be no other way to get our passports processed, I had to surrender it in the end and was relieved to have it duly returned to me, stamped by the appropriate authorities.

Rapids on the Congo River between Matadi and the capital Kinshasa meant we had to complete the next 370 kilometres by land. Early the next morning we loaded all our baggage on to the train to Kinshasa. Cloudy skies kept the temperature moderate as we travelled through the lush forest, captivated by our newly adopted country. When we arrived, I was thrilled to receive letters from WEC headquarters in England and friends in Ireland. Although excited by all the new situations I was experiencing, those blue airmail letters brought a sense of security in the midst of a very different world.

In Kinshasa we spent a few days doing necessary paperwork. As I thought of what lay ahead, I read the Bible verse on my calendar and received it as a word from God to my anxious heart: 'For God has not given us a spirit of fear' (2 Timothy 1:7, NKJV). It was followed by a quote from the famous missionary Hudson Taylor: 'Pray on and labour on. Don't be afraid of the toil; don't be afraid of the cross; they will pay well.' I tore off the page for the day and tucked it into my diary. I would need that encouragement in the days to come.

On Sunday, along with friends from the Baptist Missionary Society, we had our first experience of a Congolese church service in the Lingala language at 8.30 in the morning. Although we understood little of what was said, we were impressed with the enthusiastic worship of the Congolese Christians. The two-hour service was followed by an English service where we met several American friends and enjoyed lunch together afterwards. The whole

Sunday experience brought a warmth to my heart and a sense of normality in the midst of tumultuous change. The next morning we were up early, arranging the transport of our heavier luggage. This would travel up the Congo River to Aketi and from there by train to Isiro. We would take the easier option and fly north to Isiro, after completing our preparation courses in Kinshasa and Kimpesi. At the British Embassy in Kinshasa, we were introduced to the ambassador who gave us a pep talk about being British citizens abroad. On our journey there we drove down a road lined with endless paintings and people wanting to sell their work to the newly arrived British citizens.

Then it was time to start attending to our own work. Rhoda, Isobel and I began an eight-day *stage* (course) on hygiene at the State Institute in Kinshasa, opening our minds to the challenges of nursing in the tropics. Although we had expected heat and humidity, it was not unbearable. Rain showers cooled the air, though they also turned the dust to mud. We wore our sun hats and adapted to the climate, relaxing with the BMS girls in the evenings, and sharing meals and prayer times together.

Letters arrived for Isobel and myself from the WEC field leaders, Jack and Jesse Scholes, and from an elderly missionary called Daisy Kingdon with whom we would soon be working and learning Swahili. Jack and Jesse signed their letters 'Soli' and 'Ma Soli' respectively, the nicknames they had been given locally. The letters had been written as we arrived in Matadi, and it was touching to know our leaders were thinking and praying for us as we entered our new sphere of life.

Daisy wrote, 'How good to remember His promise, "My grace is sufficient for Thee", as you face a new land, a new language, a new people, untried ways and sometimes difficulties – but hallelujah, His grace is always sufficient and His guidance perfect.' I treasured her words and the thoughtful care behind them. I still keep those letters, in their original envelope, fifty years later.

Finishing our initial course in Kinshasa, Rhoda and I moved to do a three-week *stage* in Kimpesi, leaving Isobel in Kinshasa. This *stage* was necessary for the vital government certificate allowing us to practise medical work within Congo. Kimpesi was a large inter-mission hospital run by American Southern Baptists. We stayed in a hostel where two hostesses, Dot and Marg, looked after us with great kindness and introduced us to iced tea – I had never tasted anything so delicious, particularly after a hot day's work at the hospital.

As we began our *stage*, however, the reality of life in Congo began to hit home. Despite the good standard of the hospital, I was shocked at the lack of hygiene in the crowd of unwashed relatives milling around the patients. The compound was red with dust and raucous with voices. After a rainy night, everywhere – including the wards – was covered in mud by the morning. This was not medical care as I knew it in the UK.

It was a fascinating time nonetheless, experiencing medical work in the tropics, watching doctors battling to save patients with complex needs. We were involved in medical clinics, orthopaedics, physiotherapy, maternity work and the care of premature babies. We spent afternoons in the laboratory, helping to process hundreds of tests for diagnosis. We did not fully appreciate it at the time but in the months and years to come we would understand how important the lab work was for diagnosis.

It was also a time of contrasts. We were overwhelmed by the kind hospitality shown by mission personnel, the excellent food provided for us, the trips to the swimming pool organised so that we could relax and cool off. On one occasion we had breakfast with the Swedish ambassador and his wife who had stayed overnight. On another day we met Dr Burkitt, famous because of his identification of the children's disease Burkitt's lymphoma, which thanks to his discovery could now be treated and cured. I was thrilled to discover him a humble godly man originally from Enniskillen in Northern Ireland.

On the other hand as we went out with local health visitors we were shocked by the extent of infant malnutrition and the severity of disease in the local community. In the leprosarium we saw hideous deformity caused by leprosy while we learned about its diagnosis and different stages of treatment. Travelling to rural clinics and returning home over mud roads in a tropical storm added a further element of adventure. Almost every day our return was marked by the death wail from the hospital as another patient passed away, a sobering reminder of the challenges faced by those trying to help in this difficult medical situation.

Kimpesi gave us broad experience of life in a large hospital. We saw everything from training in the nursing school to social work in the community. On Sundays we attended the local Congolese and English church services, and on some weekdays went to sell Christian literature in the local market. I was determined to take every opportunity not only to treat physical ailments but to address the spiritual need of the people I had come to serve.

The *stage* came to an end as we said goodbye to the friends we had made in Kimpesi and received our certificates. In one final show of God's love to us, Dot and Marg got up at 4.00 a.m. on the morning we left to have breakfast with us and see us off. We returned to Kinshasa where I met up again with Isobel and said farewell to Rhoda who was leaving for her RBMU mission station. We had shared a momentous time in our lives, travelling to Africa and preparing for the work God had for us, but now we had to go our separate ways.

In Kinshasa I had time to review what I knew of Congo. A large country in the heart of Africa, it was surrounded by nine other African countries. When it declared independence from Belgium in 1960, Congo had been the second most industrialised country in Africa after South Africa, with mining and agriculture the main income sources. Cobalt, copper, diamonds, gold, silver, zinc, tin, uranium, radium, bauxite, iron ore and coal were all to be found, especially in the south-eastern region. The country was considered one of the world's richest countries in natural resources.

In 1960 Patrice Lumumba was the first leader in the country to be democratically elected, but he was subsequently deposed and executed. Joseph Mobutu took over as president in 1965 and established a one-party state in which he was in complete control. He renamed the country from its former name at independence, Republic of the Congo (Léopoldville), to the Democratic Republic of the Congo. President Mobutu also renamed the nation's cities: Léopoldville became Kinshasa, Stanleyville became Kisangani and Elisabethville became Lubumbashi.

We had arrived in 1968 when the country had a good infrastructure, with main roads well maintained by the owners of the coffee, tea, cotton and rubber plantations. These estates played a dual role, providing employment and buying goods from the local population. Banks, post offices and other essential services worked most of the time. Yet political storm clouds were rolling in the background.

Aware of this but full of enthusiasm for our next adventure, Isobel and I flew from Kinshasa up to Isiro in north-eastern Congo, where our field leaders met us. I was thrilled to finally be in the presence of Jack and Jessie Scholes, both in their late sixties, who had worked with C.T. Studd, my hero.

'Maud, how lovely to have you here. I trust that God will bless you as you settle in Congo.' Jack reached out to shake my hand, a smile lighting up his weathered face. A quiet Lancashire man, he was as kindly and welcoming as he had been in his letter and I felt privileged to be introduced to missionary work under his leadership. Jessie embraced us like a mother. Together their strong faith in God and sensitive care of mission personnel would be a bulwark against the ebb and flow of our youthful fears and emotions as we adjusted to life in Congo.

Having collected the luggage that had travelled separately, we drove through the Ituri forest in the Scholes' four-wheel-drive vehicle to the head mission station at Ibambi. Soli's Congolese driver, who went by the unlikely name of Eliza, balanced the wheels with great expertise on either side of deep ruts in the mud road. By the time we reached our destination it was 6.00 p.m., darkness had fallen and we were exhausted from our travels. The Scholes introduced us to the other staff at Ibambi, including Frank and Lily Cripps, Elaine Aitken and the Congolese staff. Schoolboys marched in parade in front of us and church leaders lined up to welcome us to Congo. We felt like VIPs.

The next morning we had the full, official welcome: parades, singing and speeches from the printing-press team, Bible-college and primary-school students. Unaware that we would be received with all these formalities, I felt embarrassed that I had not a speech prepared in reply. I would soon come to understand the usefulness of having some words ready for all occasions. That evening the other missionaries joined us for an official welcome meal hosted by the Scholes at their home.

We ate by the light of oil lamps, their soft glow reminding me of my early days on our farm in Ireland. With Ibambi close to the equator, the sun set at 6.00 p.m. and rose at 6.00 a.m. throughout the year. I relearned how to light Aladdin and Tilley lamps, with their fragile mantles. Thankfully the little hurricane lamps which we used outside were not so fragile, though the light from them was much less.

As the WEC headquarters in Congo, Ibambi boasted a health centre and maternity unit, with the main hospital being twelve kilometres north in Nebobongo. Frank Cripps had built a printing press which provided the church with a variety of booklets and literature invaluable to the local Christians. Near the printing press building was the graveyard where C.T. Studd was buried. It seemed fitting that he should lie there, at the centre of the mission he had founded all those years before.

Finally I could unpack my larger luggage which I had not seen since it left Ireland. 'Oh no! Look at this!' I could not believe the red jumble that met me. I fished out a book and held it aloft, the sticky mess dripping from it like blood from a wound.

'The tin of strawberry jam has burst over everything. How will I ever salvage anything out of this?' I glared at my laughing friends who seemed unimpressed by the extent of the disaster.

'And my sewing machine has broken too. What am I going to do?'

'Don't worry, Maud, I'll have a look at it,' replied Frank

Cripps, taking pity on me. 'At least the medical equipment has survived the journey, that's the important thing.'

Frank, who repaired everything that broke down, managed to mend the sewing machine. I learned to survive without a few other things that I had thought indispensable.

We obtained identity cards and learned to drive the Land Rover on the treacherous mud roads. One of my first driving lessons developed into taking a patient to Nebobongo and then on to Isiro for help. It was my first experience of driving in a tropical storm, with visibility limited and my control of the vehicle tenuous, sliding down into muddy gullies and struggling out the other side. It was with a sense of relief that I delivered the shaken patient to the hospital.

Isobel and I were asked to speak at the local secondary school. I was nervous, conscious of the limitations of my language and my understanding of the culture in which these young people lived. I was being stretched by demands that I felt were beyond me. At night I was restless, unable to sleep from a combination of excitement at new experiences and concern over the expectations of others. Would I be able to cope with life in this strange environment?

Fellowship, Bible study and prayer times with missionaries and local Christians were very precious. I grew used to hearing others pray in a variety of languages. Helping with practical work around the compound alternated with forays to the local market in the company of one of the older missionaries to play gospel messages over a speaker and give out tracts. As yet we spoke only French and no local language, so our personal contact with the local population was limited.

Almost as soon as we arrived, Christmas was upon us. It was of course very different to Christmas in Ireland, with no emphasis on cards, decorations, a tree or presents. What they did have was a huge church conference, *makutano* in Swahili, where all the outlying churches joined up with the main church in Ibambi. We knew the crowds were coming long before we saw them, hearing their singing and drumming from a long way off, feeling the vibrations under our feet.

And then they came, marching, dancing, playing drums, carrying pots, pans and all they needed to stay at Ibambi for a few days. The women carried everything on their back in one big cloth called a *kikwembi,* tied into a bundle and supported round their forehead. Some had baskets, carried in a similar fashion. I was overwhelmed by the joyful exuberance of these Congolese Christians. Group after group arrived on Christmas Eve, each group coming first to the missionaries' house where we greeted them and prayed with them. The day was spent welcoming all these various groups from the outlying churches.

That evening five thousand people were together, praising the Lord and singing Christmas carols. Many of our traditional carols had been translated into Swahili and were sung to the same tunes that we already knew from home. As we sang 'O come all ye faithful' and 'Silent night' with our brothers and sisters in Africa, even though we were each singing in our own language, I felt the thrill of our oneness in Christ. What a privilege to be here, all members of one Christian family.

The choirs, mostly young people, did not sleep much because they spent the night singing and parading around the houses and church, where many of them camped out. Christmas Day began with a 7.00 a.m. service, followed by others at 11.00 a.m. and 3.00 p.m., each service lasting about three hours. The sermon was preached in three languages: Swahili, Bangala and Kibudu, or another tribal language. The offering took almost an hour as people queued, singing and dancing in rhythm, to go up to the front of the church to present their offerings.

As part of the afternoon service we celebrated the Lord's Supper together, with water instead of wine. For us as new missionaries it was a different way to spend Christmas Day, but for these Congolese Christians the focus of the day was on the One who had come to earth for them. We were touched and challenged. In the evening the missionaries had their Christmas meal together: chicken and rice with spinach and some tinned ham, followed by a cake baked by Ma Soli as a special treat.

On Boxing Day another meeting in the morning brought the *makutano* to a close and people dispersed. They went back to their villages, singing and drumming, leaving an indelible picture in my mind of joyful African spirituality and my first Christmas in Congo. The oneness of the worship and the experience of coming together in praise from so many different backgrounds seemed to me a foretaste of a greater gathering to come. On Christmas evening I recorded in my diary: 'yet nothing to what will be in glory.'

At the end of December Isobel and I packed our bags once again and prepared to leave Ibambi to travel around 100 kilometres south to Wamba, where we would study Swahili with Daisy Kingdon for the next five months. Although we had some grasp of French, Swahili was more widely spoken by the local people. As someone who was not a natural linguist, my heart sank at the idea of having to start learning another language. As ever, I turned to God's promises. *'Rien n'est impossible à Dieu'* (Luke 1:37), I noted in my diary the morning we left Ibambi, using my improving French. 'Nothing is impossible with God.'

5

LEARNING

The three-hour journey to Wamba in Jack Scholes' pickup was enlivened by a number of river crossings. Often Eliza hopped out of the vehicle to repair a bridge with an impromptu arrangement of logs. As the vehicle bumped and swayed across the shifting structure, Isobel and I held onto door handles and car seats, as if to aid our safe crossing. We reached each river bank with a prayer of thankfulness for our survival. At one point, where the river was too wide for one of Eliza's bridges, we drove on to a little ferry made from planks of wood on a raft. The men propelled this construction across the river by pulling on a suspended rope. It was to be the first of many such crossings.

'Maud! Isobel! It's so lovely to have you here.' Daisy Kingdon welcomed us to Wamba, introducing us to the Congolese staff as she showed us round the primary school and health centre. 'It will be great to have your help in the health centre. This is Bobbie Andre who does so much for us.'

The young Congolese man held out his hand and smiled, his face lighting up in welcome. '*Jambo, Mademoiselle*. We are happy to have you in Wamba. God will bless you here. We will work well together.'

'*Jambo*, Bobbie Andre.' I looked into his dark eyes and warmed to his kind words.

Wamba mission station stood on top of a steep hill, looking out over the surrounding countryside; below us lay the town and the convent where Helen Roseveare and other missionaries had been held during the Simba rebellion. It was a sobering reminder of the price paid by those who had gone before us.

Our first two months were given over to Swahili language study. Daisy was a good teacher and I tried to make the most of the opportunity to concentrate on the language, knowing that soon we would be involved in medical work. Once our initial language study came to an end, my mornings were spent helping a Congolese nurse, Elia, deal with a long queue of people waiting for consultations. In the mornings Bobbie Andre worked as secretary, dealing with the many administrative tasks of the centre as well as dispensing medicines. In the afternoon I helped Bobbie in the lab so that patients would have the result of their tests by the next morning. Our friendship grew as we worked together. When we finished the lab work, Bobbie went to the forest to work in his garden until dark; like everyone else, he grew his own food. Sometimes in the evening Daisy took us out to meet the local people, giving out tracts and selling a few Christian books in Swahili.

Isobel and I shared Daisy's house, lit in the evenings by the same type of lamps as we had experienced in Nebobongo. We collected water from the corrugated tin roofs of the buildings on the compound and used a basin of water with care. When we needed an extra supply, Alphonse, the house servant, would go to the nearest waterhole and carry back what he could. My mind went back to my years growing up on the farm in similar conditions and I smiled to myself. I could do this.

I came to rely on the BBC World Service on my little radio to keep me in touch with the outside world. Through it I learned of the civil rights protests and developing trouble in Northern Ireland. In January 1969 I followed the story of the Russians carrying out the first crew exchange in space between Soyuz 4 and Soyuz 5, a feat that seemed almost inconceivable from my isolated situation in north-eastern Congo. The rest of the world was far away and space travel beyond comprehension.

In the new year I received a surprise bundle of mail from Ibambi, including Christmas cards and letters from home. My joy at receiving them was tempered by concern over news of my mother's recurring illness. Doctors seemed unable to reach a definitive diagnosis. Such issues were magnified by the distance between us and I could only pray that God would touch her physically and spiritually. At that point I began a habit of daily letter writing to keep up with all the replies I felt people deserved. These mounted in a satisfying pile until a runner came from Ibambi with mail some weeks later and took mine back for posting.

I was concerned by our lack of medical facilities. Pneumonia, malaria and worms were recurring problems. Sometimes we lost patients because of our limited resources. A little child with polio suddenly lost the power of his arm, leg and voice. I absorbed the mother's pain as if it was my own. 'What does one do here?' I pleaded in my diary. My daily prayer was for wisdom to deal with the challenges which confronted me.

I needed not only wisdom but stamina. Through the night I was on call for emergencies; during the day I had constant nursing duties in outpatients, the dispensary and the laboratory. Finding a space to continue with language study was difficult. Some days my tired brain refused to take in the Swahili words dancing on the page in front of me. Sundays were busier than other days with three consecutive services and Swahili hymn singing in the evening.

Overwhelmed by the need around me, frustrated by my lack of progress in Swahili and concerned over my mother's illness, I became weighed down by a sense of my own helplessness. What good was I accomplishing in this place? One evening I noted in my diary, 'Testing and purifying process today – if it had been possible, I would have packed my bags and gone home. But I proved His grace is sufficient.'

I was referring to 2 Corinthians 12:9: 'My grace is sufficient for you, for my power is made perfect in weakness.' The Living Bible rendition was particularly precious to me: 'I am with you; that is all you need.' I was called to follow the Lord Jesus, weak as I was, so that I would not glory in anything that was achieved but that He would get the glory. As I absorbed that truth, I never again wanted to give up although many times I longed for a break.

One particular weakness persisted. Snakes and mosquitoes I had been prepared for, but my childhood fear of mice had developed into a phobia which kept me awake at night listening to the rats running about overhead in the roof. I set traps and caught some but there always seemed to be more. I was unable to shake off this persistent fear.

One night I had been eating peanuts before bedtime and failed to tidy up before going to sleep. During the night I woke to find myself eye to eye with a rat, regarding me through my mosquito net. He was sitting on the small table by my bed clearing up the remains of my peanuts. I was almost hysterical with terror and did not sleep again that night. Living in Daisy's house, my control over my living conditions was limited. I needed God to step into the situation. I prayed that He would deliver me from this phobia of rats and mice which was interfering with my life and work.

But there were good times too. Sometimes we saw very sick patients healed as we prayed for them. One man who was convulsing and beyond all hope of recovery suddenly became calm and returned to normal as we watched and prayed. Such cases strengthened our faith and were a witness to the patient's family of the power of the God we served.

Occasionally Isobel and I managed to get away for a walk to the river to allow our brains to recover and our bodies to relax while Daisy was busy with other meetings. The flowing water brought coolness to the air and the fertile soil hosted an abundance of fresh green foliage. One day we met a Greek Cypriot who owned three coffee plantations in the area. He presented us not only with a gift of coffee but even someone to carry it home for us.

Another bundle of mail arrived. There was snow in Ireland and also in Canada where my sister Irene now lived. In my life of constant heat, it sounded very refreshing. Mother was ill again. My sister Dorothy was planning her wedding in May. I would be in Congo, missing the milestones of family life.

On 1 April I recorded in my diary, 'No human person here knew it was my birthday. But the Lord gave me a wonderful day of spiritual blessings.' Secretly I enjoyed not letting Daisy and Isobel know it was my birthday. I wanted to prove I was strong enough to survive without people having to make a fuss of me. A week later was my mother's birthday, which I spent in special prayer for her. She had now been diagnosed with ulcerative colitis. Later that month Isobel did not keep her birthday a secret and we celebrated with a chicken dinner and Christmas pudding which she had received in a food parcel from her sister.

At the beginning of May post arrived with the news that Isobel and I were to move to Nebobongo for a few months. This was exciting. Nebobongo, near Ibambi, was the main hospital for the area. Mrs Edith Moules had set up a leprosy colony there in 1940 and Dr Helen Roseveare had founded the general medical work in 1955. By this time she had moved on to work in Nyankunde but had left behind a well-developed hospital.

On our arrival in Nebobongo we were welcomed by two older missionary nurses, Gladys Rusha and Florence Stebbing. Florence had responsibility for the medical department and Gladys the maternity unit.

'How much experience have you in maternity?' asked Gladys, leading the way to the maternity department.

'Not a huge amount. I went to MTC straight from my midwifery course.' I felt inadequate already.

'We have to do all kinds of obstetric procedures here that would normally be done by a doctor in the UK. You have to be prepared for anything.' She frowned as she surveyed the ward, packed with pregnant mothers, new babies and attendant relatives. 'So much can go wrong and mothers often turn up when it's too late, ending up with a dead baby or a ruptured uterus. Now I think we have a breech ready to deliver in here. Follow me. You'll soon expand your skills – forceps deliveries, twin births, ventouse deliveries; we have them all.'

My heart sank at the thought of the challenges ahead.

In the afternoon Florence introduced us to work in the pharmacy. 'Don't worry, you'll soon get the hang of it!' she grinned, handing us each a glass container. 'We make up all kinds of potions and solutions in here. Antiseptics, anaesthetics … we can do anything.' She looked round the pharmacy until her eye caught the box she wanted. 'Here we are! Iron crystals! This afternoon we'll make some tonic water.'

'Tonic water?' I queried. I was unfamiliar with the term.

'Great stuff!' she laughed. 'So many people are anaemic. This is the answer.' Mesmerised, Isobel and I followed her instructions. Pharmacy work with Florence promised to be interesting.

Although more limited than the medical centre at Kimpesi where we had done our initial *stage,* Nebobongo was a full hospital with surgical, medical, maternity, and outpatient departments as well as a busy leprosy camp. We saw the progressive and permanent damage of nerves, skin, limbs and eyes caused by leprosy. Research into effective treatment was still under way. Risking their own health, Gladys and Florence cared for these leprosy patients who were isolated from others because of the risk of infection. As we assisted and observed, we saw not just their medical expertise but their trust in God and their love for the people of Congo.

When God first called me into full-time work, I thought it would mean giving up my nursing to concentrate on evangelism and preaching. As soon as I arrived in Congo, however, I saw the great need for medical care, and at Nebobongo I realised how many opportunities it presented for sharing the gospel. We held a service every day in the outpatients department as patients waited to be seen, surrounded by their families. Time spent with mothers in the maternity department as they anticipated a birth often gave rise to conversations about the God in whom we trusted. In a situation where resources were limited and our help finite, missionary and patient looked together to the Lord for help.

We quickly settled into a busy routine in the hospital, with each day's demands of ward rounds plus pharmacy and lab work. Alongside my nursing duties I tried to keep working on my Swahili but long hours and many demands left me discouraged by my lack of progress. I clung to the promise God gave me from Mark 9:23: 'Everything is possible for one who believes.'

My times with the Lord at the beginning of each day were a priority to keep everything else in perspective. I noted in my diary at this time, 'How fresh and precious is my dear loving heavenly Father's word each morning.' To make sure that happened, however, meant an early start. One morning I observed, 'Rather annoyed with myself for sleeping in till 5.45 a.m.'

From time to time our usual routine at the hospital was enlivened by visiting surgeons, who came for a few days to perform surgery beyond our limited abilities. One was the seventy-five-year-old American Dr Becker, based with Dr Helen Roseveare in Nyankunde. A tall, scholarly missionary working with AIM, he had devoted a lifetime to the people of Congo. The doctors usually flew in on an MAF (Mission Aviation Fellowship) plane to an intensive schedule, speaking at services around the hospital and spending long hours operating. We were always sorry to see them go, with all their news, encouragement and medical help.

Letters came from home, including one from Aunt Maude describing my sister Dorothy's wedding and my mother's continuing illness, which forced her back into hospital the day after the wedding. These family concerns tugged at my heart and reminded me of my commitment to follow God's call whatever it meant. I had left home and family and was rejoicing in the opportunity to fulfil God's plans for me, but the human ache of separation remained.

At this time God provided a welcome break from the relentless hospital routine and my inner struggles. WEC missionaries Jim and Ida Grainger were driving from Ibambi through Uganda to visit their son who was teaching in Kenya. They offered to take Gladys Rusha, an English missionary, and myself along for the trip. Exactly a year after I first arrived in Kinshasa, we set off, stopping at WEC stations along the way. On the Sunday morning we arrived in Nyankunde, situated in grasslands above the rain forest. At the church we received a warm welcome and I was delighted to meet Dr Helen Roseveare for the first time. She was in the process of starting a nurses' training school in Nyankunde while Dr Becker was setting up the clinical side.

After some time in Nairobi with the Graingers, Gladys and I left them with their son and spent some time with Bill and Marion Finch at the Scripture Holiness Mission in Londiani. Their situation was very different to ours in Congo; running water and electricity made it a refreshing and relaxing stay. I had the opportunity to speak at the local girls' school through an interpreter and rejoiced to see a number of them put their trust in the Lord.

While we were there I received the first letter I had had from my mother since leaving Nebobongo three weeks before. It brought distressing news: my dear Aunt Maude had died suddenly as a result of a heart attack. Once again the cost of being away from home at such a time struck me. I had been close to Aunt Maude since I was very young and she had had a significant influence on my life. Although I knew she was with the Lord, the thought of not seeing her again on this earth brought great sorrow.

On our way back to Nebobongo we stopped in Nyankunde for a medical conference where Helen Roseveare was one of the speakers. Her word brought balm to my aching heart. The event was also significant for the impact political attitudes were having on our work in Congo. For the first time African delegates were taking the lead in the conference. The balance was changing as missionaries handed over more responsibility to African colleagues.

Back in Nebobongo I returned to my normal duties. One morning I was woken at 1.20 a.m. by loud banging on my door. It was Isobel. 'Maud! Sorry to wake you. We've just arrived. Any hot chocolate?'

Having been in Nyankunde for a month, she had travelled back by road with Helen Roseveare. Although they had been driving since 5.00 a.m. the previous day, we sat up drinking hot chocolate and talking together until 4.00 a.m.

I was somewhat in awe of Helen's reputation in WEC and nervous about talking to her. While I had met her briefly in Nyankunde and listened to her speak in public, this was the first opportunity for us to have any in-depth conversation. As soon as she came into the house, however, she put me at ease. Friendly and chatty, she helped me forget my inhibitions and over the next few days we enjoyed long discussions together. My previous awe was replaced by a deep affection and I found our time together encouraging and inspiring. From that visit in January 1970 a friendship began that I valued throughout the years ahead.

Helen had come for the Ibambi missionary conference. Following the Nyankunde medical conference, African church leaders were invited to be part of the Ibambi conference for the first time as the mission tried to integrate with the Congolese church. Learning was taking place on both sides. The attempt to overcome any feelings of segregation was beginning as discussions took place together rather than separately.

Helen had a great overall vision for the work of WEC in our area of north-eastern Congo, which was about the size of Great Britain. At the conference she presented the idea of having a main hospital in the north and another in the south as well as the existing one in Nebobongo which would be halfway between. Around each main hospital would be a network of smaller rural dispensaries. At the time this seemed an immense plan but it would eventually come to fruition.

At end of that conference missionary postings were announced. With our initial language study and medical orientation completed, Isobel and I parted company. Isobel was to go south to Mulita with the Graingers. Jim and Ida had set up a Bible school there and Ida, a nurse, had an extensive leprosy camp and a health centre where Isobel's help would be valuable.

I was to return to work with Daisy in the health centre in Wamba. I had peace that this was where God wanted me to be. When I discovered that £100 had been sent from Ireland earmarked for transport, I realised it would cover my moving costs. The Lord had provided and confirmed His plan. I was ready for the next stage.

6

A TURN IN THE PATH

The clear voice of the lead singer soared in a short phrase, echoed by the surrounding choir. African harmonies rose in the air, bodies swayed and hands clapped. The beat of the drum led the rhythmic pounding of feet. Dust swirled around the ankles of the dancers, obliterating the pattern on the lower half of their skirts as they moved in time to the music. It rose to where we sat in the front row, breathing in heat and dust, the air of Africa.

I was back in Wamba, where Daisy Kingdon had introduced Isobel and me to the Swahili language the year before. Elaine de Russett, an Australian nurse, was leaving as I was arriving, so a special *makutano* was being held to mark both occasions. Jonah Atibasai, the local headmaster, orchestrated the parade as hundreds of children marched past in school uniform, church choirs sang and danced, and the enticing smell of cooking chicken hung over the proceedings.

The head pastor, Danga, fatherly and gracious, thanked Elaine for all she had done and welcomed me to Wamba. Atibasai was quick to add his contribution, full of enthusiasm for all that we would accomplish together. Elaine and I spoke in reply, appreciating their kind thoughts. When she was a young nurse, Elaine had been captured and held along with Helen Roseveare in the Simba rebellion. Now she was being honoured by those who understood her love for the people of Congo. As the official proceedings drew to a close, women presented us with generous plates of food. *Sombe* (a dish made with the cassava leaf) and rice were the staples but chicken cooked in palm oil with onion and tomatoes, as only the Congolese could do it, was the highlight.

Once again I would be based mainly in the health centre. With Daisy and myself the only two missionaries, we would be relying on the help of our Congolese colleagues. Daisy was now walking with the help of a stick because of arthritis but was held in great respect in the local area.

The days settled into a pattern. Each morning at 6.30 a.m. we took it in turns to lead a Bible study and prayers in the church. The morning Bible study was important as some of the Christians did not have Bibles or could not read. As we met together, they learned to apply biblical truth to their lives and grew in their faith.

Bobbie Andre was a great help in the little gospel service we held for the patients later each morning before our clinic. With my limited experience, clinic consultations were daunting and kept me relying on the Lord for wisdom. Elia, the Congolese auxiliary nurse, ran a clinic for patients left over from the morning clinic while I helped Bobbie Andre. He and I were delighted to be working together again, processing samples in the laboratory each afternoon.

My Swahili was still somewhat rudimentary for public speaking but I soldiered on with study when I could fit it in. Later in the day I held knitting and sewing classes for the girls. As they acquired these practical skills, we talked about the Lord, His word and what He could do in our lives. A kids' club gave both boys and girls an opportunity to hear the gospel as they listened to stories and sang choruses together.

In the evenings, if we did not have a church or committee meeting, Daisy and I would often go walking in the local area, down the main road that led towards Kisangani and up the avenues leading off it. As we made our way through the small mud houses roofed with soft wood tiles or with leaves and grass, we stopped to talk with the men sitting around in groups, discussing the affairs of the day.

The women were preparing food outside their homes, tending the cooking pots balanced over a fire on a circle of bricks or stones. As the sun went down and the air cooled, the smell of *sombe* and rice mingled with smoke from the fires. In between tending their cooking pots and chasing off inquisitive chickens, the women were happy to chat to us too: '*Jambo, Mademoiselle. Habari yako*?'

They greeted us with a smile, enquiring how we were, under no time pressure with meal preparation. Those times of conversation with the people living around us were important as we formed a bond with the local community. For those who could read, we had a supply of Christian books.

Relationships with our Congolese colleagues were also important. Some evenings we had prayer and fellowship meetings with our African leaders, which kept good communication between us. The evenings when the vivacious headmaster Atibasai came to visit were full of fun as he shared stories from school along with his godly wisdom. As a school teacher, Daisy loved to hear of the school's progress.

I shared Daisy's house. She had been there for a number of years and ran her household efficiently, in charge of what we ate and the two house servants who prepared the food. Each morning we had porridge made from Quaker oats which we obtained from Isiro. We made our own bread with yeast and used powdered milk. We were blessed with a plentiful supply of fruit. Bananas, papaya and avocados grew locally. Daisy was very proud of the strawberries which she grew in the garden and were otherwise unobtainable.

Wamba was surrounded by coffee and tea plantations, mostly owned by Greeks who sometimes came to us for medical help. They reciprocated by helping us out with transport when needed. We gave them Christian literature and looked for openings to present the gospel.

While I appreciated the abundance of fruit, the juiciness of Daisy's strawberries and the aroma of fresh coffee, my heart sank when I entered the house in the evening to the smell of pilchards. Dinner was usually rice with pilchards or sardines. With little choice of meat, we needed the protein these provided, but the sight and smell of them made me shudder. Sometimes we had beans or corned beef as an alternative but the pilchards reappeared often enough that I would never be able to eat them again.

One day a great fuss erupted outside our house. 'Davie and Isude are here! God has delivered them! They have come back to us!' People were calling to each other in excitement.

'Who are they? Where have they come from?' I was bewildered.

'They've been gone for six years. We thought they would never come back. Here they are.'

In the midst of the crowd I saw a bedraggled little family enveloped in an emotional welcome.

Gradually their story began to emerge. Before the 1964 rebellion, evangelist Davie Malamu had travelled north with his wife and family to evangelise and preach. On the outbreak of trouble, they were captured and taken into the forest by the rebels. The eldest daughter was being forcibly imprisoned to become the wife of her captor when a tall figure dressed in white robes appeared, walking towards them. Terrified, their enemies ran into the forest, allowing the girl to return to her family. The figure then disappeared. Giving thanks to God for sending an angel to deliver them, the family took cover in the deep forest. As they were so remote, they had no idea when things in the outside world became safe for them to return.

On another occasion God gave Isude a vision of impending danger, in which she saw rebels coming to the place where they were staying. Next morning the family moved to a different part of the forest. They later heard that the rebels had indeed invaded the area where the family had been living, destroying all in their path.

Despite all their difficulties, they continued to trust God and even conducted services in the forest. Many came to know the Lord through their witness. Food was almost non-existent; they survived by eating berries and hunting animals when they could find them. When their clothes wore out in the forest, they replaced them with bark-cloth.

Three years after their captivity, God gave them the gift of a baby son. Some people in hiding abandoned their babies in the forest because of the danger of the baby's cry letting the rebels know where they were. But Davie and Isude trusted God to protect them and their newborn child. When they found their way out of the deep forest and back to Wamba, I considered it a privilege to care for them medically in our little health centre. God challenged us all as we listened to their story and praised God with them for His deliverance.

In the remoteness of our situation we often had the opportunity to see God at work in miraculous ways. One day a child was brought to the health centre, convulsing and severely ill. Discovering it was the result of roundworms in his young body, we treated him with rectal chloral hydrate, a sedative medication slowing the activity of the central nervous system, and gave him liquid piperazine rectally in an attempt to kill off the ascaris roundworms. These treatments would never be used now but it was all we had. Greatly concerned for this young life, we prayed much over him. By the next morning he had made a dramatic recovery and in a couple of days he was completely well. Thrilled by his miraculous recovery, his parents put their trust in the One who had intervened to save their child.

Sometime later another young boy, around nine years old, was brought to the health centre, suffering from cerebral malaria. His father was a teacher at the school in Wamba and both parents were committed Christians. Standing round the boy's bed, we prayed with them for their son's recovery. Slipping in and out of consciousness, he suddenly spoke clearly: 'I can see Jesus. He's telling me to come to Him.' As we continued to pray, he went to be with the Lord he loved. It was not easy to understand why some were miraculously healed while others were taken. We lived each day holding onto the One who had brought us to this place, who knew all about the challenges we faced and whose ways are perfect.

When I arrived in Wamba, Daisy had encouraged me to start a maternity work, given the great need for women to deliver their babies safely. Our African *chef de poste*, who wore several hats as an evangelist and as head of the mission station alongside the pastor, worked very hard and organised the building of a maternity ward.

Unable to access supplies locally, I sent to England for the necessary equipment. The instruments I ordered from England in June 1970 had still not arrived by March of the following year.

We were almost ready to open the maternity ward when one evening Dauda, our 'runner', came to me with a letter from home marked 'URGENT'. Fearing the worst, I tore open the envelope. It was a letter written by my youngest sister on behalf of my father. My mother had had a stroke and was seriously ill in hospital. My father, never convinced about my missionary choice, now wanted me to come home. I had received a number of letters about my mother's ill health but always trusted that God would heal her. This time seemed to be different.

'She is not going to recover,' he wrote. 'I cannot care for her, and as a daughter and a nurse it is your duty to be here.'

I was devastated. I hated the thought of abandoning my mother when she was so ill and yet I was just getting to grips with what I felt was my life's work in Congo.

I remembered the talks we had received in Missionary Training College in Glasgow, with the warnings of those who went to the mission field and were unable to survive their first term. I thought back to my Aunt Maude's talk about not giving up on my nursing training, no matter how hard it became. Giving up was the last thing I wanted to do.

In MTC I had always said to myself, 'No matter what happens, I'm going to stick out my first term. Even if it kills me, I am not going to give in. I'll stay the full term.'

I had clung to this principle through all I had experienced so far in Congo. Was it possible I was letting a principle get out of proportion to the overall situation? What was the right thing to do? I was facing one of the hardest decisions of my life.

I shared my dilemma with Daisy and together we decided I should go and see the Scholes, our field leaders, to discuss the situation. The morning I left to go and see them, I prayed that the Lord would give me a verse of Scripture as guidance for the way forward. That particular morning in my Bible reading I came to the story of God speaking to Jacob in a dream: 'I am with you and will watch over you wherever you go, and I will bring you back to this land' (Genesis 28:15). God's word to Jacob jumped out at me. He was telling me not only that I had to go, but also that He would bring me back to this land again. He had given me a similar promise when I left Ireland to come to Congo.

Feeling that this word was from the Lord, I was able to share it with the Scholes, who understood the situation and agreed I should go home. Without that promise, I do not think I would have gone. But accepting His word to me and the confirmation from our field leaders, I was able to let go, hard as it was, and accept it as His will. It was May 1971 and I had served almost three years of my five-year term.

As soon as my plane touched down in Belfast, Willie Weir, the WEC representative in Belfast, met me and took me straight to Magherafelt hospital to see my mother.

Willie was from my home town of Cookstown, so he knew my family and understood the situation. While I was overseas he had been a great encouragement as a committed letter writer. On the way to the hospital he entered into some of my inner turmoil over leaving Congo and my concern for my mother.

My mother had originally been diagnosed with ulcerative colitis but they had now discovered she had inoperable cancer. She had been getting blood transfusions from time to time but it transpired that the stroke had been caused by a secondary tumour in her brain. Shortly after my return she was discharged to my younger sister Dorothy's house but she was not happy there, so we brought her home to her own bungalow.

Over the next three months I cared for her through the pain of that final illness. Although she had not opposed my going to Congo, I never really knew up until this point where she stood spiritually. Every evening when I was getting her ready for bed, I would ask if she would like me to read the Scriptures and pray with her. She was always very quick to agree. On two particular occasions, when I felt she was too weak and tired, I did not do it. On both occasions she said to me the following morning, 'You forgot to read and pray with me last night. Now don't forget tonight.' That meant a great deal to me. Although I was unsure previously of her spiritual standing, the word of the Lord was more meaningful to her than any medical help I could give her. That was a confirmation to me of her relationship with the Lord and of the rightness of my decision to return.

In August my mother passed away and my intention was to return immediately to Congo. My father, however, had other ideas. Twenty years older than my mother, he was unable to look after himself but was unwilling to go to live with either of my married sisters. He had never expected my mother to die first. It was hard on him and hard on us as a family to know what to do. He wanted to stay in his own home with me there to look after him. Frail and in his eighties, I knew his life was limited so felt I should stay and care for him.

Shortly after my mother died, I met the assistant matron in Magherafelt hospital. 'Would you consider coming to help us in outpatients, even part-time?' she enquired. 'We're really short staffed.'

'I have no intention of going back to nursing,' I explained. 'I'm hoping to go back to Africa soon.'

'What about three weeks?' she asked. 'Even that would help us.'

Three weeks seemed possible, so I agreed to it. At the end of the three weeks, the arrangement was extended for three months, after which I was asked to help in maternity for six months. Working in Magherafelt hospital with those experienced midwives was very useful as I had gone straight from nursing training into Bible-school training, without any nursing experience in a UK hospital. When a vacancy came up for a district nurse around Cookstown, I took the post, realising it would be more convenient than Magherafelt and closer to my father.

One experience stands out from my time in the Cookstown district. A young married man with small children was terminally ill with cancer. I was giving him nursing care, which included injections twice daily to relieve his pain. One morning I asked him if he would like me to read the Bible and pray with him, to which he gave an enthusiastic response. I read John's gospel 14:1–7, which included these words: 'Do not let your hearts be troubled … I am going there to prepare a place for you … I am the way and the truth and the life.' Afterwards I prayed with him. That evening he asked me to read and pray again, which I did. Sensing an unspoken request, I asked him if he would like to trust the Lord Jesus as his Saviour. His response was unequivocal: 'Oh yes.' I will never forget the sense of God's presence in the bedroom that evening as I led him in prayer. He immediately spoke to his wife and she too accepted the Lord as her Saviour.

Next day his mother came to visit him; she did not live in the Cookstown area and was unknown to us. We discovered she had been praying for her son for years and was overjoyed to hear the good news. A week later he passed peacefully into the Lord's presence. My experience with this young family was one of the highlights of my time in district nursing.

My father remained resistant to my Christian faith but I read Scripture to him and prayed with him regardless. One morning I read the twenty-third psalm to him and said, 'Wouldn't you like to know the Lord as your own personal Shepherd?'

He nodded his head in reply. 'Yes, I would.'

There in his own home, where he had held out against the gospel for so long, I had the joy of helping him come to Christ. It was a wonderful answer to prayer.

When my father died a few weeks later, it was a great relief to know that he was with the Lord and a privilege to feel I had had a part to play in pointing both my parents to the Saviour. Contrary to my expectations, my father had lived for seven years after my mother died. Despite my initial reluctance to return from Congo, I could see with hindsight that God had worked out His plan during those years at home.

The door to Congo opened for me once more.

7

NEBOBONGO SAFARIS

My second journey to Congo, now renamed Zaire, was very different to the first. This time I knew where I was going and who I would be working with when I got there; I travelled by air rather than sea. Robert Mackie, the international director of WEC, was planning a trip to Zaire as part of his role in visiting all our mission situations, so I was delighted that his visit coincided with my return journey. We arrived in time for the WEC missionary conference in January 1980, where Robert spoke to us from God's word and decisions were made about the way forward before he returned to England.

I would be working in Nebobongo. The welcome from both Zairois and missionaries was warm and familiar, easing my transition back to Africa. My larger luggage, following me from Ireland, did not travel quite so smoothly, arriving exactly a year later.

I moved into a little brick house with Beryl Shannon from Canada, who looked after the hospital books and finance as well as running a Sunday school and children's work. A young English couple, Tony and Dr Sylvia Hare, were heading up the work in Nebobongo, with their infant daughter, Julie, and a second child on the way. Florence and Gladys were still there, although Gladys was preparing to go on leave.

Thanks to the excellent grounding I had received from Gladys in local maternity work, I would take over the maternity unit. With no resident anaesthetist, I was also called upon to administer anaesthetics while the surgeons operated. 'I can't possibly do that,' I protested. 'I know nothing about it and have never attempted such a thing. There is no way I can take on the responsibility.'

'It's amazing what we can do with God's help,' responded Dr Westcott, an American UFM doctor who came from time to time to do more major surgery. 'We all work way above our training and expertise here. If there is no one else to do a job, don't you think God will equip you?'

Reluctantly I had to agree. Gentle and reassuring, Dr Westcott led me through the technicalities of anaesthetics and helped me extend my skills as needed. Much prayer ascended from the operating theatre while I found my way into another new role.

Alongside the learning of new skills, I was relearning my French and Swahili after the long break in Ireland.

Tension returned with a familiar tightening of my stomach muscles. How could I balance a heavy workload with the time and energy needed for language study? When would I be able to communicate clearly and fluently?

The hospital had progressed since I was there nine years before. All the wards were now brick buildings and a generator produced electricity for the operating theatre. Diesel oil to run the generator was expensive and difficult to obtain so its use was restricted. Tony, ever practical, installed the first solar panel on the roof of his house, producing enough power to give light as well as recharge batteries for the radio transmitter and radio cassette recorder. Convinced by the success of this experiment, I ordered a panel for our little house, largely replacing the need for expensive paraffin oil for our Tilley lamps and batteries for radio cassettes and torches.

Our two nurse-surgeons, John Mangadima and Asea Palo Andre, had been trained to do emergency surgery by Dr Helen Roseveare, Dr Westcott and others. John co-ordinated the medical work while Asea was the hospital director. Every day we had at least one emergency operation. Patients arrived with strangulated hernias of two or three days' duration, requiring a resection of the bowel. Mothers came in obstructed labour, needing immediate intervention. My life fell into a routine, working at the maternity unit and operating theatre, doing ward rounds and helping with medical consultations. Leprosy and public health work still awaited my attention.

The practical Dr Westcott had a gift for appropriate technology. During his times with us he built an autoclave and sterilising room plus various useful extras such as a large cement sink. He came every six weeks, alternating with others. He always brought his sense of humour, introducing fun as an antidote to the stressful situations in which we found ourselves. He had great rapport with the African nurses, giving them excellent training in surgery. My fellow countryman Dr John Kyle from Newcastle in County Down, who headed up Nyankunde hospital at that time, also came occasionally to do surgery. An eye consultant came less frequently. The arrival of any of these doctors heralded a busy ten days or two weeks but their help was very much appreciated.

As well as the ongoing medical work, we tried to serve our outlying churches by doing surgical safaris when we could, usually about every three months. Some, completely isolated in the forest, had no medical facilities within reach. Either John Mangadima or Asea would accompany me on these safaris. A female helper also came to look after sterilising and practical work, leaving one of the nurse surgeons in Nebobongo. We would do more than 100 operations in a week, working from 6 a.m. to 6 p.m., except on Sundays when we were invited to preach in the local church. We prayed with each patient before we operated and often had opportunities to talk to them about their faith.

One day when we flew into a clearing in the forest, we were surrounded by an excited crowd. '*Mademoiselle*, our brother was caught by a crocodile in the river.'

'*Mademoiselle*, look at his arm. The crocodile had it in his teeth.'

'He is very sick. Can you fix his arm?'

As we looked at the mangled arm, we knew the semi-conscious patient was beyond our help. It was obvious from the smell and appearance that he really needed an amputation. We did our best to explain. 'We cannot help him here. We do not have the right equipment. We will put him on the plane back to Nebobongo. They will help him in the hospital there.'

Convinced by our explanation, the patient and family members boarded the plane and set off for Nebobongo.

It was always sad to hear of people who had died since our previous visit, often from preventable causes, but with the nearest hospital beyond reach there was nothing that family or friends could do. The choice was to let patients die at home or try to carry them long distances, perhaps 100 kilometres or more, to find medical help. Sometimes a feeling of helplessness came over me, faced by the enormity of the need which we could not meet. Yet I knew the real need of the people was spiritual. It gave us great joy in these remote areas to be able to share the gospel message with those who had never heard it and to encourage those who were seeking to follow Christ.

It was a new experience for me to live and eat in African homes, with occasional rebellion from my digestive system. We worked in primitive conditions, with our operating theatre a mud hut, whitewashed in an attempt at sterilisation, and our spotlight my big torch. We brought all the packs, drugs, instruments and autoclave we needed with us from Nebobongo hospital.

About four months after I arrived in Nebobongo, John Mangadima and I decided to respond to a request from the church in Opienge. This was a village 100 kilometres into the forest from the main road, about 420 kilometres from Nebobongo. The last missionary there had been the WEC missionary nurse Winnie Davies. In this isolated spot deep in the Ituri forest, Winnie had built up a thriving medical centre and a primary school with qualified teachers. At that time in Opienge there were a few Greek stores served by four Greek families, many African shopkeepers and a Roman Catholic community centre served by three European priests.

Winnie arrived to work there in 1955. Nine years later she was taken by Simba rebels and held in the forest for thirty-three months. While she was in captivity, no one outside the country knew where she was but the Congolese Christians loved her and suffered to protect her. A Dutch Roman Catholic priest, Father Strijbosch, who was in captivity with her, was eventually rescued by the army. He revealed that the rebels had killed her in the forest just a few minutes before their rescuers arrived.[2]

After the rebellion not a building remained standing on the mission station; all were demolished and the materials carried away. But the Christians had not wavered, and were determined to rebuild what was lost.

In 1980, when John Mangadima and I were planning to visit, there had been no medical work in Opienge since Winnie's death. From time to time African church leaders had come out on foot for church general assembly meetings, walking over 100 kilometres and bringing news of the situation. The church was still together, led by the faithful Pastor Alieni, but there had been no outside help since Winnie Davies died.

On 8 April we flew into Opienge by MAF plane. The pilot delivered us with our luggage, including everything we needed for our stay, confirming that he would return for us after a week. We followed the pastor down the path to his home where we would sleep, a small mud house with a grass roof. I had brought my own camp bed, little sponge mattress and mosquito net in order to avoid sleeping on the hard *karagba,* the bamboo bed usually provided for visitors. The village was made up of the church, a little health centre and a collection of mud houses in the forest.

We knew there would be much to do and were unsurprised that hundreds of patients awaited our arrival. We operated, used up all our anaesthetics and medicines, and packed up to go at the end of the week. We had no radio or other means of communication but were confident that the plane would return for us as agreed. On the assigned day we made our way to the airstrip with all our luggage, listening for the drone of the little plane's engine. At the end of a long, hot day of waiting, we had to accept that the plane was not coming. So we made our way back to Pastor Alieni's house, unpacked our bedding and settled down for the night. Next morning we packed up everything once more and took it all to the airstrip, sure that the plane would come that day. After another day of waiting and hoping, there was no sign of the aircraft.

For the next four days we packed and unpacked everything each day in expectation of the plane's arrival. Eventually we decided there was no point in sitting there waiting every day. We still packed up daily in case a plane would come but we stopped taking everything to the airstrip. Instead we tried to make the best use of our time by concentrating on helping as far as we could with an outpatients clinic and in church, preaching on Sunday.

One Sunday afternoon the local Christians took us on a long journey over some frightening one-log bridges. They wanted to show us a wide waterfall, under which so many Christians had been able to hide during the Simba rebellion. It was fascinating to stand there in the spray and imagine both the terror of those fugitives and their gratitude to God when He delivered them.

On the Monday we heard a plane coming and got very excited. We gathered up our possessions and ran to the airstrip with camp beds, equipment and all our luggage. The plane swooped low but climbed again without landing. We waited, thinking the pilot was checking out the airstrip, then watched in dismay as our hopes disappeared with him into the sky.

We discovered later that rather than it being an MAF plane, it belonged to the Okapi Wildlife Reserve which covers around one fifth of the forest. That area of Congo is the only place in the world where the okapi, or forest giraffe, is found. An endangered species, its habitat is threatened because of logging and it is hunted locally for bushmeat. A very rare peacock, the Congo peafowl, is also only found in the reserve. We knew that national park planes sometimes flew over to monitor these rare creatures but, focusing on our predicament, were still confused and dismayed not to be picked up.

We trekked back to the village once more. By now we were beginning to wonder if we would ever be collected. Church members told us about a Roman Catholic mission station some distance away. The priest there had a radio transmitter; under normal circumstances we could have gone there to contact Nyankunde and find out what was happening. However the Pope was visiting Zaire just at that time and the priest had gone to Kisangani to see him, so that means of contact was ruled out.

I kept listening in on my own little shortwave Sony radio, thinking there might be a local broadcast about the plane delay, but there was no mention of it. Two weeks went past, and still no plane. As the days stretched into weeks and the waiting continued, we could not understand why we had been left seemingly abandoned in the forest. The time crept up to three weeks and I was beginning to get desperate. We could not exist in the heart of the forest indefinitely. We decided we would have to try to walk out and began to make plans for the journey. Our hosts, however, were dismayed at the prospect and discouraged this, having seen my fear of single-log bridges on the day we went to the waterfall. 'You'll never be able to do it, *Mademoiselle*. It is well over

100 kilometres to the nearest road. You have to cross rivers without any proper bridges. It's too dangerous and difficult for you. You'll never make it.'

What was I to do? I had very little choice. I was ready to do anything to get out of the forest and knew that somehow God, who had brought me to this place, would care for me whatever happened.

Three weeks and one day passed. I was helping to do an antenatal clinic when we heard another plane. By this time we had had so many disappointments that we did not get too excited. Thinking it was the national park plane again, we went to the airstrip without our baggage. We really did not expect the plane to be for us.

This time, unbelievably, the plane circled, then came in to land. The MAF pilot jumped down from the cockpit and grinned. 'Well, did you enjoy your holiday?'

I was flabbergasted. 'Some holiday! What happened?'

'Be honoured, you're the first flight for over two weeks. Both planes were down. We had to send to the United States for the needed parts and then go to Kinshasa to collect them.'

They had come for me first, prioritising my flight because of the remoteness of my situation. On reflection I was grateful, realising there were folk from AIM and UFM also waiting for their flights. The relief was overwhelming as we packed up our baggage and boarded the plane, thankful to our hosts who had cared for us during our extended stay but looking forward to being back home in Nebobongo.

Nevertheless the sense of isolation and the anxiety surrounding the whole experience was indelibly seared on my mind. As a result of this incident, a rule was introduced by the mission that no one would go to a remote area in future without some means of communication. Radio transmitters and solar panels to power them were ordered for outlying mission stations.

I arrived back in Nebobongo to discover that Jesse Scholes, Ma Soli as we all knew her, had died from a heart attack while I was stranded in Opienge. I was distressed to find her gone. Her husband Jack, Bwana Soli, had died in 1971 and she had soldiered on in Ibambi. When I left to go on the safari, she was talking about doing some painting in her house. I offered to do it for her when I returned but she said, 'No, while you're away, I'm going to do the painting.' Eighty years old, she was a wonderful lady with a caring heart and a strong faith. Along with Bwana Soli she had welcomed Isobel and myself into their home when we first arrived in Ibambi in 1968. Their loving welcome left a lasting impression on us and I mourned her passing.

A short time later Dr Westcott was forced home to the United States for medical treatment. Everyone was sad at his departure as he had done so much, not only for Nebobongo but also for the whole of north-eastern Zaire over the years. Although in poor health and nearing eighty years of age he said to me on leaving, 'Watch out, I might be back if there is no one to fill the gap.' It was a great sorrow to hear of his death later in the year. He had brought not just his surgical and teaching skills but his deep faith in God and sense of joy in serving the people of Zaire. We all missed him.

We prayed desperately for more doctors and nurses, and particularly for an eye specialist. Eye diseases were widespread in the area. The answer to this prayer came in an unexpected way. A voluntary organisation in England, Sight by Wings, undertook to send us an eye specialist every six months. The first to arrive were Professor and Dr Fisher from St Mary's Hospital, London. They gave us a laugh as they bantered together. On one occasion, when I was distressed that dinner had burnt while their operating list stretched longer than expected, Prof. Fisher reassured me in his lovely Oxford accent: 'Don't worry Maud, carbon is good for flatulence.' Their loving and friendly personalities encouraged us and we were grateful for their practical help and ministry.

In August 1982, two and a half years after arriving in Nebobongo, I had my first proper holiday. My friend Isobel Purdy, another WEC missionary who had worked in Nebobongo but was now living in Nyankunde, invited me to stay with her during a medical conference. For two weeks I enjoyed the luxury of hot and cold running water and electricity at the flick of a switch. Nyankunde was so well developed we called it 'little America'. Coming from Nebobongo, I felt I was re-entering civilisation as I enjoyed cold drinks from her fridge and made use of her washing machine.

Back in Nebobongo there was great excitement at the arrival of new MAF missionaries, Andy and Jan Briggs, with an MAF plane. Delighted as we were to have them, this necessitated more building, not just a house for the Briggs but also a hangar and fuel reservoir. The little plane at Nebobongo would now serve the whole WEC church area, from Malingwia in the north down to Mulita in the south. As roads continued to deteriorate, this was a tremendous help in the transportation of mission personnel, food, equipment and medical supplies as well as opening up access to local Christians deep in the forest. However the cost of funding all this transport was a constant challenge. In May 1984 the economy of the country had devalued 500% since the previous October. This meant that all imported goods, including fuel, shot up in price.

Towards the end of 1984 I had been in Zaire over four years. WEC had changed the length of service for personnel from five years to four so it was time for me to go on leave. My Land Rover, second-hand when I got it and having travelled several thousand kilometres over atrocious roads, had, unsurprisingly, a cracked chassis, broken axle and innumerable other complaints. In Ireland I set about purchasing a new one to replace it. Little did I know the drama that lay ahead.

8

MULITA

Before I returned to Zaire I received a letter that would have a significant impact on the rest of my life. Jim Grainger, our former field leader, had died suddenly from a heart attack. His wife, Ida, remained in Mulita, a remote village in the heart of the rainforest. Our new field leaders, Randy and Deanna Harrison, wrote to ask if I would consider joining Ida in Mulita.

I was happy to work anywhere, as long as I was in the centre of God's will. However a new Land Rover would be arriving for me, hopefully not too long after I arrived in the country. It made sense for me to stay in Nebobongo until the vehicle arrived and then I could drive it down to Mulita.

Three Land Rovers were being imported together: one for me; one for Dr John Harris who was doing leprosy work at Nyankunde; and one for an American WEC missionary, Kent McIlroy. As soon as the Land Rovers arrived at the port of Mombasa, four of us flew down to drive them back to Zaire: a Zairian driver for John Harris's Land Rover, Kent and I to drive our own vehicles, with a spare Zairian driver, Palo, to help as needed. We spent ten days dealing with bureaucracy before starting out on the long road journey through Kenya and Uganda to Zaire.

We drove in convoy, with me bringing up the rear. Fifteen kilometres out of Mombasa, I felt the Land Rover pulling and realised I had a flat tyre. A quick search revealed that I had no jack to deal with it; in the process of packing the vehicles and rearranging the baggage, my jack had been put in one of the other Land Rovers. Although Palo was with me, we could do nothing without a jack. The others, oblivious to our situation, continued on for a number of kilometres before realising that we were no longer behind them. By the time they understood that we were missing and returned to find us, we had lost precious daylight hours on the road. We changed the tyre but John Harris's driver had arranged to meet a friend in Nairobi and was upset that we were now running late.

We set off again, with this driver leading the convoy and myself in the middle. The lead driver pushed the pace to the limit, driving much too fast for the road conditions. Embarrassed to be the reason for the delay and determined not to keep him any later, I kept close behind him, though I knew I was driving too fast. Also, in the rush to get on the road again, I had omitted to fasten my seat belt. I intended to put it on as soon as we were driving but, with the pressure of keeping up with the speeding vehicle ahead, forgot all about it.

The road was peppered with large lorries transporting goods between the port of Mombasa and the city of Nairobi. Although they were travelling at speed, sometimes with two lorries driving close together, from time to time we pulled out to pass them. The road was in poor condition: the tarmac was broken up with potholes and falling away at the sides where the tarmac had eroded. We were in danger of not only hitting one of these large potholes at speed but also of getting caught on the wrong side of the road facing oncoming traffic as we tried to push past the lorries. Gripping the steering wheel like a vice, every muscle in my body tense, I concentrated on keeping the vehicle steady on the road.

For 120 kilometres we drove as fast as possible, passing one lorry after another. Suddenly, as we were passing the second of two lorries, I thought, 'This road is very eroded on the right-hand side.' Terrified of going off the edge of the tarmac, I turned my steering wheel in an attempt to stay on the road, not realising I had already gone off the eroded side. I caught the lip of the tarmac at speed and the Land Rover went out of control, careering into the bush. If I had let it continue into the bush, it would have ground to a halt in the undergrowth, but instinct made me turn back towards the road again. We hit the edge of the tarmac once more, then with a bounce the Land Rover left the ground and turned over and over. As we rolled, seemingly in slow motion, I felt the impact each time we hit the earth. I thought, 'This is me going to heaven. Lord, I'm ready to go. If I've done anything wrong, forgive me.'

The vehicle rolled three times and came to a standstill on its side. For a moment I lay there, stunned, listening to silence, then realised I could still move and I could see no blood. I thought, 'This is a miracle, there's no blood and I'm still alive.'

I called out to Palo beside me but there was no response. My heart seemed to stop. I panicked. 'Oh my goodness, I've killed him.'

In desperation I called his name: 'Palo!' No answer.

I shouted louder, 'Palo! Palo!'

Suddenly he spoke, '*Mademoiselle,* can you open my seat belt?'

I was never so glad to hear a human voice. With trembling hands, I managed to get his seat belt undone and somehow we clambered out of the vehicle through the space where the windscreen had been.

The windscreen was on the other side of the road; the contents of the Land Rover were scattered in all directions. People stopped to help us. An English lady who had Coca Cola insisted that I have a drink. As we tried to explain what had happened, shock overcame me and I began to cry, unable to control myself. Palo, stoic and embarrassed at my reaction, said in Swahili, '*Mademoiselle*, pull yourself together.'

Kent, coming behind us at a more sensible pace, did not arrive for some time and was horrified to find us on the roadside. Throwing an arm round my shaking shoulders, he held me tight. 'You were going far too fast and I didn't want to drive at that speed in my new Land Rover. That's why I was so far behind,' he explained.

'I know you're right but I didn't want to hold the first driver back any further. I'm so sorry.' My tears were a mixture of shock, embarrassment and relief at being alive.

'I understand, don't worry about it. You were doing your best. You'll be alright now, Maud. You need to go to the hospital and get checked out. I'll take care of everything here.'

He turned to an Asian family who had stopped to offer help. 'Would you be willing to take Maud and Palo to the hospital in Voi?'

The family gathered us into their car and drove us to Voi while Kent waited for the police to arrive at the scene.

By this time my face was swelling up, my head was throbbing, and I was feeling sick and dizzy. In Voi hospital they did X-rays and investigations, ruling out fractures or serious injuries. With the aid of some painkillers, I had a few hours' sleep and at some point towards the next morning noticed that Kent had replaced Palo beside my bed. The next day doctors confirmed that neither Palo nor I had sustained any serious injury, although the Land Rover was damaged beyond repair. They discharged us to continue our journey.

While I was in the hospital, Kent had sent someone to bring back the driver of the first Land Rover so that they could put the contents of mine into the two remaining vehicles. Leaving the remains of my Land Rover in the hands of the police, Kent settled me into the front seat beside him for the journey to Nairobi. Still suffering from shock, I kept my eyes closed the whole way, unable to look at the road or at things Kent tried to point out to me. All I could see was the accident replaying in my mind like a horror movie on repeat. In Nairobi he took me straight to the Wycliffe guest house where we were well known.

There I recuperated for two weeks, allowing the others to drive on to Zaire. Bruising made it difficult for me to negotiate the steps to the guest house but the time in Nairobi allowed me to recover physically and emotionally until I could face the flight back to Zaire. The Lord reminded me of the experience of Job who lost everything and responded, 'The LORD gave and the LORD has taken away; may the name of the LORD be praised' (Job 1:21).

One of the hardest things I had to do was to ring home and tell my family, especially my sister Margaret and my minister, Trevor Coburn, that I had had an accident and that the Land Rover was a write off. I was devastated for all those who had contributed to the buying and transportation of the vehicle which I had managed to destroy on its very first road journey. Of course they were understanding and glad that I had come out of it alive but my distress lingered after the bruises healed.

Leaving Nairobi, I took an MAF plane to Nyankunde and then on to Nebobongo. As we flew over Zaire, a rainbow appeared in the sky alongside the plane. It stayed beside us as the little plane jolted its way over the country to which God had called me. It was as though the Lord was saying to me, as He had said to Noah, 'Never again will I allow you to go through such an experience.' The sense of God's presence and the reassurance that He understood all the emotions I was experiencing brought comfort to my soul.

The embarrassment I felt on returning to Nebobongo without the Land Rover was dispelled by the sympathetic and loving welcome given by staff and friends there. Dr Sylvia Hare and her husband, Tony, were kind and caring, and their two little girls helped to lift my spirits. In many different ways they helped me overcome the humiliation of the accident and encouraged me to thank God for my deliverance and look to Him for the future. He still had a plan for me in Zaire.

Trying to put the episode behind me, I finally managed to get an MAF plane to Mulita. On the first attempt we were halfway to Mulita when we were met by an impenetrable blanket of cloud just over the equator. The pilot decided it was safer to return to Nebobongo.

The next available MAF flight was nine days later. We packed the plane with medicines and my personal luggage, but as the pilot was doing his final pre-flight check, he received an urgent call to a medical emergency. We unloaded the plane once more. As it took off without me, I began to wonder what God was doing. The Christians at Nebobongo were saying, 'See, the Lord does not want you to go to Mulita.'

On the following day, 16 May 1986, we finally flew into Mulita, where we arrived to a tremendous welcome with singing and dancing. Disregarding the feelings of their brothers and sisters in Nebobongo, the Christians in Mulita kept saying, 'The devil was trying to stop you getting to Mulita. Thank God that He had the victory.' I was touched that both groups of people wanted me in their part of the country and amused at their different interpretations of events.

An isolated clearing in the forest, Mulita lies in the province of Maneima, Zaire's least populated, most isolated and possibly poorest province. When I arrived in 1986, it was very different to the buzz of Nebobongo. Chimpanzees called from the forest and sometimes were to be seen playing on the airstrip. The almost constant rain brought the croak of frogs and the chirp of crickets. In the drier season the song of weaver birds replaced that of frogs. I never tired of watching their suspended nests bouncing overhead as they built their intricate structures. Situated a few kilometres from the large Lowa River, Mulita had white sandy soil, unlike the red soil of Nebobongo.

Most of the hospital consisted of mud, stick and leaf-roofed buildings which lasted for a limited period and constantly needed to be replaced. One small brick building served as the health centre and was used as a pharmacy and outpatient department. The leprosy department was a separate collection of mud huts almost a kilometre away from the main hospital. In those days leprosy was still contagious, so isolation was vital.

Another collection of mud huts made up the Bible school, giving accommodation for students along with one small brick classroom. There was also an incomplete brick church building and a little mud primary school with no qualified teachers.

Ida was living in an old brick house which she and Jim had built. By the time I arrived the walls were dilapidated and the thatched roof disintegrating. When it rained, we had to put basins under the leaks to catch the water streaming in. Joy Taylor, who had been in Mulita with Ida until a short time before, had started building a new brick house but work had stopped with her departure. I moved in with Ida as a temporary measure, with a view to finishing the new house.

From our neighbours' houses, smoke escaped through roofs and doorways and hung in the air. The smell of smouldering wood will always evoke for me the smell of Africa. The local people cooked in an outside kitchen or just in the open air, over stones around a fire. Occasionally folk would cook inside their hut, but there was always the possibility of the leaf roof catching fire and going up in flames.

Sometimes people would come from the forest area with dried meat to sell. It was usually some kind of bushmeat they had killed, perhaps monkey or antelope, dried after a fashion but smelling dreadful by the time it reached us. Similarly smelling fish was offered for sale at the market, brought from Lake Albert up to the north between Uganda and Congo. Loved by the local population but shunned by those of us not used to it, we referred to this Makiabu fish as 'Mucky eyeballs'. Attempts to preserve it left it with a very salty taste. Our diet tended to be mostly vegetarian.

By the time I arrived in Mulita I was feeling at home in Zaire, although I had not lived in such an isolated situation. However the large number of leprosy patients was new to me. With little experience of working with leprosy, I had to learn quickly. Ida and I went every day to the leprosy camp to dress the sores that afflicted the patients. As we undid bandages, the smell of rotting flesh rose around us. Sometimes in the morning we met people with new sores from rats eating their feet at night while they slept; with no feeling left in their extremities, they had been oblivious to what was happening.

For the first five weeks I had the privilege of working with Ida until we went back to Nebobongo for a medical conference. Ida had agreed to sell her Land Rover to Ibambi missionaries, so the Harrisons came to Mulita on a MAF plane for a supervisory visit and then to drive the Land Rover to Ibambi with Ida and myself. Now well into her seventies, Ida felt God was leading her to retire and return to Australia. The main question was whether I should stay on my own in Mulita. It was the most remote and furthest south of the WEC mission stations and since the 1964 rebellion no missionary had worked there alone. The Harrisons were uneasy about the situation. At the medical conference we discussed it at length.

'It's not a good idea for you to be in such a remote area, with no other missionaries nearby. If you are in trouble, we have no way of knowing,' they argued.

I understood that they felt responsible for my wellbeing but I felt sure of God's leading. I visualised the secluded village in the forest, with people coming from a distance for medical care and Bible school. 'I have only been in Mulita a short time but I have the assurance that it is the right place for me. It's a strategic place, with great need, and the local church wants me to stay. If God wants me in Mulita, He will look after me.'

'Alright, let's try it for three months until you come back here for the missionary conference in January. Take as little luggage as possible so that we can evacuate you if necessary.'

'That's fine. I'll leave all my household things here in Nebobongo. The church have promised to look after me in Mulita with whatever I need.'

Delighted, I made plans to return to Mulita. I would not be completely out of touch as I would be able to communicate by radio with other missionaries who had radio transmitters. The nearest would be the Wycliffe missionaries at Lubutu, about 120 kilometres from Mulita, although they were not always there. When they were away, the nearest missionaries were at Kisangani, 400 kilometres away.

I left Nebobongo with some African friends. Not having our own vehicle, we had to get a 'paid lift' from Kisangani to Mulita in an overloaded pickup with no windscreen. We had two flat tyres on the journey and numerous stops each time the rain came on. I was very glad of the overnight stop at Lubutu where Wycliffe missionaries Paul and Barbara Thomas provided us with a hot meal, bath and bed for the night. Next day the rain stopped so we made better progress, although the rivers had swollen with all the rain. The driver and I had to cross the big Lowa River in a canoe to ask permission from officials on the other side to use the ferry for the pickup. We finally arrived in Mulita as darkness fell, grateful to be safely home.

Despite my isolation, I was surrounded by a warm and friendly community who adopted me as one of their own and saw that I was well protected and cared for. The local people were mostly from the Kikumu tribe who on the whole lived peaceably with the three or four other tribes in the area.

I was already used to living without electricity or running water. Cooking was done by a helper in the outside kitchen, using a metal-topped brick stove with a fire underneath. An oil drum on its side, with a hinged lid as a door, provided an oven in which we baked bread. A bigger barrel over the fire was an effective way of heating water for washing. On Sundays, when no helpers were working, I had a one-ring, paraffin-oil stove on which I cooked for myself.

The pit-latrine toilets we used were fine when constructed in the right way. We encouraged carpenters to make wooden lids with handles to put over the hole at the top of the latrine. When these were not used properly, or when the latrines were not dug deep enough, an evil smell tended to linger around these buildings.

My all-important radio transmitter was powered by a car battery. This was kept charged by a solar panel unless rain hid the sun needed for this. Living on my own, I was very conscious of God's presence and saw Him provide for my needs in amazing ways. On one occasion, when I was running low in paraffin oil for my lamps, a businessman stopped to deliver some mail. He was making his monthly trip to buy palm oil from local people along our road and offered to bring me paraffin next time he came through.

Paraffin oil may have been a small need but a vehicle was a greater one. When family and friends in Molesworth Presbyterian Church and the wider Cookstown area heard about my accident, their immediate desire was to replace the Land Rover. Within six months they had bought a new one and sent it out. I was very grateful to Kent McIlroy who went all the way to Mombasa to collect it and did that whole journey again: driving back through Kenya and Uganda to Nebobongo, negotiating dangerous roads, treacherous rivers and difficult border officials.

In January I went north to Nebobongo for our missionary conference as planned. Having satisfied our field leaders that I could cope alone, I returned to Mulita with my new Land Rover. Dr Graham Cox, accompanied by his wife, Linda, and their two young children, helped me drive it through Kisangani to Mulita, around 1000 kilometres from Nebobongo. As medical director of WEC, Graham was able to visit four health centres on the way and do a medical inspection when he eventually arrived at Mulita.

The Cox family returned to Nebobongo by MAF plane and I settled into life in Mulita once more. Despite the difficulties in getting it there, I was delighted to have the Land Rover. It gave me a new sense of independence and made a huge difference to the help we could offer surrounding villages and people trying to get to our hospital. Thankful for God's protection and provision, I looked ahead with anticipation for what He had in store.

9

PROGRESS

The stark statistic of maternal deaths was the primary concern in Mulita. The church leaders presented their request: 'So many of our mothers are dying in childbirth. Can you train more midwives?'

I agreed that training others to help would be the best way forward. We had a number of auxiliary nurses whom I could train as basic midwives. The head-nurse, Kabondo, was trained in minor and emergency surgery. I arranged for our second nurse, Taabu, to go to Nebobongo to be trained also. Korosso was our specialised leprosy nurse. With no doctors around, these men would be my main helpers in the days to come.

I went to inspect the so-called 'hospital' where the midwives would deliver the babies. Newly built when I arrived, the mud huts had the usual mud floor. I looked at my staff in disbelief. 'How can you wash a mud floor? It's impossible with the amount of blood you have on a floor during childbirth or surgery. Let's see what we can do.'

We laid a layer of planks over the mud floor and covered them with plastic sheeting but it proved impossible to keep clean. 'This is not working,' I decided. 'We have to have a proper brick building with a cement floor that can be washed, and a proper roof and ceiling to keep the rats out. We can't have these rats coming in through the leaf ceiling.'

Convinced by my logic, the community rose to the task. Church leaders appeared at my door with two small brick machines. 'We have kept these hidden in the forest since 1960. They are still working and make two bricks at a time.'

'Excellent. We can use the clay from these big anthills around the compound. It will take a long time to make enough for a building but we can do it.'

We learned to make bricks two at a time in the brick machine. After drying in the sun, the bricks were built into a kiln with three triangular tunnels running through it. Into this we put firewood and kept the fires going for three or four days until the bricks were fired and durable.

Over the brick kiln we erected a shelter, supported by four long poles, making the structure as high as possible. The leaf roof kept off the rain and allowed smoke and steam from the bricks to escape. As the bricks baked, the steam grew less. When we saw no more smoke or steam but only heat shimmering above the kiln, we knew they were ready.

At the beginning we made many mistakes: not drying the bricks long enough before firing them, not firing them long enough and sometimes putting too many in the kiln itself. However we learned by our mistakes and eventually bricks began to grow into a satisfying pile.

Brick making provided work not just for those who fashioned the bricks from clay but also for those who gathered firewood from the surrounding area and those who kept the fires going until the bricks were ready. It was a community project, with the women who came to the weekly antenatal clinic bringing one big stone or two smaller stones for the foundations each visit. We dug and laid the foundations but prayed for patience. The building was held up due to a lack of cement. Road conditions needed to improve before we could get the necessary building materials from Kisangani. In the meantime we built two more temporary mud wards until we could get brick buildings constructed.

John Anderson, an architect from my church in Cookstown, drew up a plan for the maternity unit which impressed the authorities. Very slowly the buildings began to take shape. We prayed constantly for wisdom and skill as none of us were building experts.

God brought us people with some experience in building. Theodore, a gracious Christian man and an elder in the church, was experienced in felling trees and cutting up the wood into useable planks. Theophile, our head carpenter, was also a godly man, very gifted at teaching the younger ones. An older man, Cornei, had been taught by the Belgians to do masonry work, so was useful in training others to build.

One day a young man came to my attention. A patient in the hospital, he had recovered from his illness but had no money to pay for his treatment. I looked at him with a smile. 'It's not a problem, Ibeyo. You can work to pay off your medical bill. What would you like to do?'

'I would like to help with the masonry work.' He looked eager. 'I have done building before.'

'That's great,' I said. 'You can help us build the new hospital.'

Ibeyo turned out to be a skilled workman who learned quickly. We took him on to pay off his debts but because he worked so well he became a permanent member of our workforce.

The thatched roof of the Graingers' house was at least ten years old and could no longer be repaired so I concentrated on completing the 'new' missionary house, which had been under construction for the past six years. It needed cement floors and the tin roof was leaking badly but we managed to repair most of the major leaks. I moved in on Christmas Day. A new tin roof eventually replaced the old one in the spring of 1989.

While building of the new maternity unit was under way, I began teaching student midwives in the existing mud building. We used a Swahili book Helen Roseveare had written to train midwives in Nebobongo. A skilled artist, Helen had included detailed diagrams and beautiful illustrations of human anatomy. Alongside learning this theory the students attended weekly antenatal clinics. Whenever a patient arrived for delivery we all left our books and went to maternity to see what was happening. In this way their training was constantly practical. When I first arrived, the hospital depended on me for all complicated deliveries, but gradually the midwives built up their experience and confidence.

Mama Betissa, a large lady with a loud voice, had been a local midwife in the forest, learning from her mother who did the job before her. Because of her background, church leaders had employed her to work in the hospital before I arrived. I went to see her in action.

'*Jambo, Mademoiselle,*' Mama Betissa greeted me. She was tidying up after a delivery although the mud hut limited what she could do.

'How do you manage?' I enquired, regarding the grubby walls and floor with misgiving.

'It's fine,' she said. Lifting a basin of bloody water, she threw it out through the window at the back of the building.

I was horrified. 'We can't do that. We'll have to find a proper way to dispose of everything.'

Mama Betissa became my first student. Despite her years of experience in the village, she was keen to learn how things were done in the hospital. With her authoritative bearing, she commanded respect from the other students who obeyed her without question. These were young girls leaving school or the wives of male nurses, most of whom had some primary-school education. I encouraged them to make notes from our classes and they learned to write up charts and birth certificates.

Far from feeling lonely with no other missionary around, I thrived on the opportunity to focus on all that needed to be done. However I was not invincible. My old fear of rats continued in Mulita. I had put down rat poison and traps over the years but somehow those four-footed friends pursued me wherever I lived. I could cope with a major crisis, knowing God would see me through, but when a rat appeared, all reason seemed to go out of the window. One in the house at night meant little or no sleep.

Now that I was on my own I determined to deal with the situation. I had prayed for God's deliverance from this phobia but I was still overcome with terror at the thought of sharing my house with a rodent. I thought of Paul and his 'thorn in the flesh' which persisted despite his prayers. Perhaps God was teaching me to use my own initiative. One day I acquired a cat. An obvious solution, she became an important member of the household, taking care of the undesirable visitors. Sometimes God provides a very practical answer to our problems.

While medical work was the main focus of my time, I was constantly aware of the spiritual need. I seized any opportunity to share the gospel message with patients, encouraging the hospital staff to do likewise. It was always a joy when someone decided to follow Christ but I also wanted to inspire them to spread the good news that they had received.

The Bible school was an important means of equipping committed Christians to reach out to the surrounding area. Staffed by a highly respected Congolese director and two or three other full-time teachers, as well as part-time staff, it offered a three-year course to those wishing to undertake church work. When the director asked me to teach Old Testament to the third years, I was delighted. I enjoyed doing the research for my classes and felt I received as much from it as the students.

On Monday nights we met in the church building where the Bible-school students shared their experiences in churches over the previous weekend. It was encouraging both for the students and for those of us listening to hear of their work in various aspects of church life and practical evangelism, equipping them for their future ministry.

On completion the students obtained a diploma and became evangelists, often in a more remote area. Once they proved their perseverance in following God's call and their suitability for ministry, they received a certificate allowing them to work as a pastor in their own church.

With days filled with hospital, building and Bible college work, evenings were the time for meeting together. Committee meetings of various sorts usually did not finish until 9.30 p.m. The medical committee meeting took place once a month and never finished before 10.00 p.m. because there were so many matters to discuss. Any evening free from an official meeting was taken up with people who called to visit.

On Sunday nights a few friends that I was particularly close to came to my house for Bible study and prayer. In the flickering light of the oil lamp, to a background choir of crickets and frogs, we had a meal and enjoyed time together. Spiritual friendship and shared experiences deepened our relationship.

Cooking was uncomplicated, with rice and cassava the staple crops, grown and eaten by everyone. Most people cooked *sombe* every day of the year, made by wilting the cassava leaf over heat, pounding and cooking it with palm oil for about an hour, then flavouring it with salt and hot pepper or sometimes peanuts for added protein. The cassava root, resembling a parsnip, was boiled to make *mahogo*. The basic diet of *mahogo* and *sombe* was sometimes accompanied by corn on the cob or rice, depending on the season.

Previous missionaries had planted fruit trees around Mulita, so I had the advantage of guavas, avocados, lemons and grapefruit in the garden. Bananas were plentiful but not mangoes, which needed a climate drier than our rainforest conditions.

A Saturday evening Bible study, which we took turns to lead, brought together all those involved with the medical and construction work. Meeting in my home, we had a time of sharing and praying together. We then finished with tea and banana bread which was very popular. With social interaction a priority in African culture, these meetings were important for our working relationship as well as spiritual fellowship.

One evening our meeting was interrupted by a call to the maternity department. '*Mademoiselle,* can you come? There's a lady here who has had three sections before and needs another one now but we have no nurse surgeon. He has gone to Punia.'

'Fine, I'll be with you in a few minutes.'

When emergencies occurred, I had to drop everything and go. Excusing myself from the meeting, I went into my bedroom and prayed as I always did before answering these calls. 'Father, you have said, "… go into your room, close the door and pray to your Father, who is unseen. Then your Father, who sees what is done in secret, will reward you."[3] I claim your promise this evening. Go with me as I go to the hospital.' I knew I was only called if the situation was serious.

When I made my way to maternity, I found the baby's head high up, not down in the pelvis as it should be. I laid hands on the distressed mother and prayed with her. As I kept my hands on her abdomen, I felt the baby's head descend with each contraction, until she eventually had a normal delivery and a healthy baby. With her history, it was a miracle. I returned home praising God once more for answering my cry for help.

Each day I tuned into the BBC world news on my little shortwave Sony radio to keep in touch with the outside world. I usually got into bed while listening to the 10.00 p.m. news, then switched it off and fell sleep immediately. Sometimes I fell asleep without switching it off which was a disaster in the days before rechargeable batteries.

With no electricity we were very conscious of the moon. I loved watching it grow bigger throughout the month, giving us increasing light at night. Around the time of the full moon, children stayed out playing, singing and dancing late into the evening, their houses silhouetted against the sky, bright with stars and moonlight. When the big moon disappeared, all became quiet; people stayed in their houses in the evening or sat around fires. Unable to afford paraffin oil for lamps, many of the local people made do with an old pot or sardine tin containing palm oil and a little bit of rag as a wick. People went to bed soon after it grew dark, certainly by 9.00 p.m., and rose early, usually around 5.00 a.m.

We started a preventative medicine programme and opened several more leprosy clinics in the area. Sometimes patients came to my door rather than going to the hospital, knowing that if they had no money, I could not send them away. I got into trouble with the medical staff for treating them on the spot. 'You should not be treating them because then the hospital doesn't get money for that treatment,' they complained. I agreed with them in principle.

The following week a Bible-school student appeared at my door, holding his baby son who was convulsing with a high fever. Even without a stethoscope I could hear his little chest rattling and knew that he was having trouble breathing. '*Mademoiselle,* can you help?' The father's face was distorted with grief. 'We have no money for the hospital but I'm afraid he's going to die.'

'Let me see him.' I reached for the child. 'He looks as though he might have pneumonia. Come in.'

I gave the baby liquid paracetamol, sponged him down to lower his temperature and started him on some antibiotics. Then I held him up before God and prayed for his recovery. The relieved father left clutching follow-up medicine.

Too late I remembered my agreement with the hospital. Next time I would give the student money and send him to the hospital. He could always repay me by working afterwards.

In February 1988 our head nurse, Kabondo, left to return to his former lifestyle. A skilled nurse, surgeon and administrator, he found some temptations difficult to resist. This was a great blow to me. However Taabu returned from his training in surgery at Nebobongo and Nyankunde just when we needed him.

Unfortunately Taabu also, like Kabondo, proved a disappointment. As his work began to deteriorate, we tried to encourage him to follow the Lord. However he did not take our advice and eventually gave in his notice. The church agonised over this but decided to accept his resignation, even though it left us without a surgeon in between surgical visits from Nebobongo. In an emergency we had to rely on staff who had picked up the basics from assisting nurse surgeons in the past but we took patients requiring surgery to Punia.

When we were most aware of our lack of expertise, God's enabling power carried us through. Sometimes mothers were brought in with ruptured uteruses from childbirth, or men came with strangulated hernias after cutting down trees in the forest. After surgery in Punia, they often made good recoveries and went back home praising God for His saving and healing power.

I was due to go on leave in November 1989 so for the last six months before I left concentrated on finishing as many projects as possible. In the leprosy camp the little mud church and dispensary needed replacing with brick and cement buildings. The leprosy patients were finding it impossible to keep up with the constant repairs to their own mud houses as well as the mud church and dispensary buildings. As with the other buildings, we began by collecting stones for the foundations, then made the necessary bricks and sourced the other building supplies.

I had kept in touch with Dr Helen Roseveare since that first meeting in Ibambi, and while she was still in Zaire I met up with her most years at the annual missionary conference. Though at this stage she was living in Northern Ireland, in 1989 she came to Zaire for the making of a film on her life there. This film, *Mama Luka Comes Home*, was being made on the twenty-fifth anniversary of the Simba rebellion. I invited her to come and perform the official opening of our leprosy centre buildings before she left.

This was an exciting event for the whole community who were pleased and honoured to receive her. Helen was accompanied by Margaret Collingwood from BBC Bristol, who was co-ordinating the making of the film. The buildings were opened with much celebration, giving the leprosy patients an enhanced sense of worth and easing life for them in terms of building maintenance. Helen spoke words of encouragement, impressed with our building programme, slow though it seemed to me.

With my leave coinciding with the end of their stay, the plane which came to collect Helen and Margaret took the three of us to Nairobi. There Margaret treated Helen and myself to beautiful African dresses before we caught our respective flights back to the UK.

As I journeyed home, I reviewed what we had achieved in terms of construction. The maternity building had made good progress and the builders were preparing to put on the roof as I left. We had replaced the tin roof on my new house, laid a cement floor in the main Mulita church and completed the leprosy camp buildings. We had also rebuilt the administrator's mud and stick house as well as maintaining the general upkeep of all the other existing buildings. Church and community had worked hard to get six mud and stick classrooms ready for the opening of a little primary school. The Bible school now had three classrooms to house each of the three year grades. The two new classrooms were only buildings of mud and stick until we could manage to replace them with brick buildings.

But I was conscious that my main reason for being there was deeper than constructing buildings. More significant, but more difficult to assess, was the spiritual work done by the Lord in the hearts of the people. A big encouragement before I left was to see both our nurse surgeons, Kabondo and Taabu, come back to the Lord. Having repented, they asked if they could return to work. For the present we decided to accept only Kabondo. For the first three months he would go to Nebobongo and Isiro to be under the supervision of our missionary doctor Graham Cox and the church president Pastor Mazaburu. I prayed that both Kabondo and Taabu would follow the Lord wholeheartedly and return to work in Mulita.

The work would be left in Zairian hands during my absence. Nurse Mwendeni was left in charge of the medical work and Mama Betissa in charge of the maternity work. I was confident that our church leaders would continue to care for the people spiritually. As I travelled back to Ireland, I thanked the Lord for all those He had raised up in Mulita to continue to share His love with the people there.

10

UNWELCOME INTRUSIONS

In August 1990 the new maternity building was taking shape as planned when I arrived back in Mulita. The need was more evident than ever, with some mothers walking forty or fifty kilometres to reach us. Our head nurse and surgeon, Kabondo, was back, helping with the medical work once more. A much-changed person, with a new desire to serve the Lord, he was an invaluable asset in our busy hospital.

The Bible-school students were busy building a mud and stick house for our new Bible-School director, Ikabu, who arrived with his wife, Idey, and family three months after my return. Idey had trained as a nurse and midwife in Nyankunde so I was looking forward to her help in the maternity work while Ikabu took over responsibility for the Bible school.

Late one afternoon I was called to maternity and went across to the hospital, leaving the door of my house unlocked as usual. During the day there were always people around and guards on the compound so I never locked the door. Having dealt with the situation in the hospital, I returned home as dusk was descending and headed to the bathroom for my 'bucket bath'. Before my house help left, she always heated water over the fire and brought it to the bathroom. Standing in a plastic basin of warm water and throwing it over myself with a small container was quite an efficient way of washing, now that I had grown used to it. I dried myself off and looked around for my torch which seemed to have disappeared. Thankful for the solar panel lighting which was now functioning, I prepared some fruit salad, my usual evening meal, and read for a while before putting out my light around 10.00 p.m. as usual.

I woke around midnight to the sound of a voice. At first, heavy with sleep, I thought Amisi, the night guard, was talking to someone outside. As the sound continued, I realised it seemed closer, as if it was in the house. Reluctantly I opened my eyes, as if that would help me hear better. The outline of my closed bedroom door was illuminated and there seemed to be a light flashing on and off in the living room.

Carefully I inched my way out of bed and opened the door. A man was wandering round the living room by the light of my torch, talking to himself. I was not sure if he had a mental problem or was on drugs but something was wrong. In any case he should not be in my house in the middle of the night. With some indignation I demanded, 'What are you doing here?'

He turned towards me, a white woman in a nightdress outlined in the doorway, and smiled. 'Ah, my wife. We need to go to bed.' Taking my arm he headed into the bedroom.

My heart pounded with fear, all the local stories of attack and rape sweeping through my mind. I was alone and unprotected. Shooting off an urgent prayer for help, I accepted his pressure on my arm and turned him round towards the back door. 'Yes, that's fine but let's just go to the door for a breath of fresh air first.'

He followed my lead and together we walked to the door which I flung open as I yelled for the night guard: 'Amisi! *Unisaidia*! Help!'

Amisi was already in the outside kitchen near the back door. Seeing the torch flashing and hearing voices inside, he had realised something was not as it should be. He made a grab for the intruder who twisted out of his grasp and ran off into the darkness.

We called the pastor who came immediately. Together we drank tea and talked about the incident, deciding that the man must have gained access to the house while I was at the hospital earlier. Now that he was gone, my heart rate returned to normal and I thanked God for my deliverance. I went back to bed but there was no more sleep that night.

The next morning a hunt was organised for the man, who was discovered in Mulita graveyard about half a kilometre from my house. He managed to escape again by crossing the River Lowa in a canoe, about six kilometres from Mulita. He was high on drugs and had probably been looking for more in my house, or the money to buy them. It was a sad situation for his family who lived in a village just outside Mulita and for his father who was a catechist in Mulita church. Years later he repented and came to Christ, renouncing his drug addiction and becoming involved in the church. However I could never look at him without reliving the terror of that night.

Such incidents were thankfully rare and I focused on the development of the hospital. With the opening of the new maternity department, the patient numbers increased far beyond our expectations; we were almost immediately short of beds. Although often overwhelmed by the pressure of caring for so many, we found the women very open to the gospel and had the privilege of helping many of them put their trust in God. The state medical officer was so impressed with the maternity building that he encouraged us to build a surgical ward to replace the existing mud, leaf-roofed building. Even he could appreciate that the latter was not the most hygienic environment for post-operative patients.

The Leprosy Mission had asked us to expand the region in which we worked to cover the whole Maniema province. I therefore appreciated the arrival of the German Leprosy Mission nurse Roswitha Mann in January 1991. We were now responsible for a large area where Roswitha would set up new leprosy clinics and supervise existing ones.

L-R: Dorothy, Margaret, Irene and Maud, July 1945

Maud in RVH uniform, 1963

En route to Congo on board the Lumumba October 1968.
Isobel, Maud and Rhoda worshipping with others on Sunday

Land Rover stuck on a log bridge

Bicycles had to be carried over a log bridge

New maternity department, Zaire

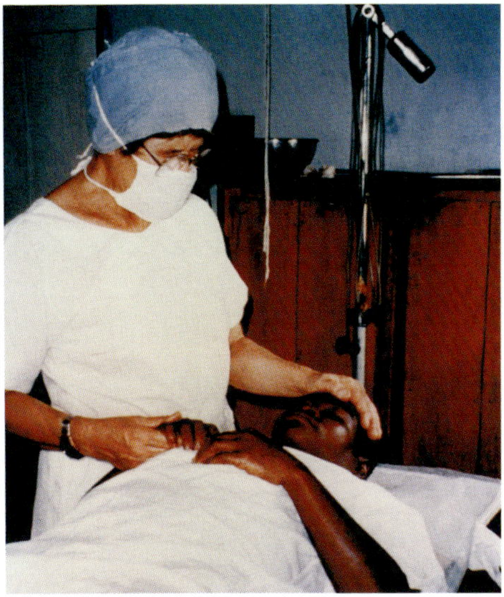

Maud praying with patient before surgery

Transporting everything by bicycle after the Land Rover was taken

Crossing Lowa river

Unloading medical supplies from the MAF plane at Mulita

Maud preaching at Mulita makutano, Christmas 2012
(Inset) Twins born on Christmas day

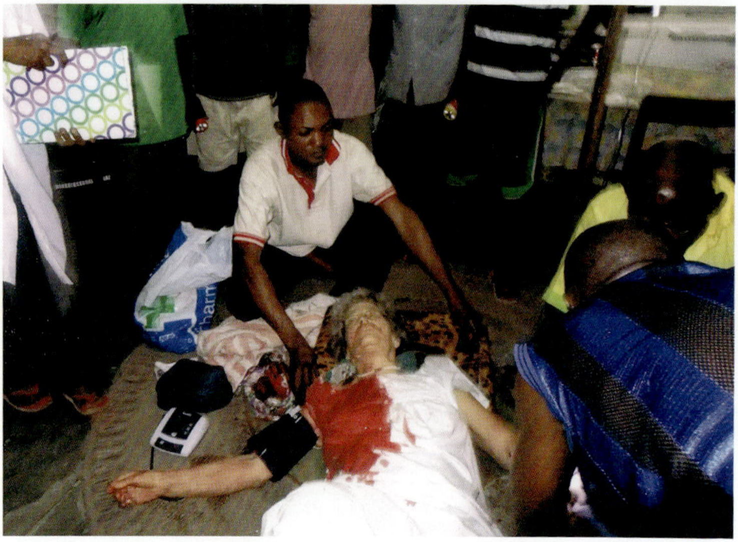

After shooting incident, 4 Jan 2015

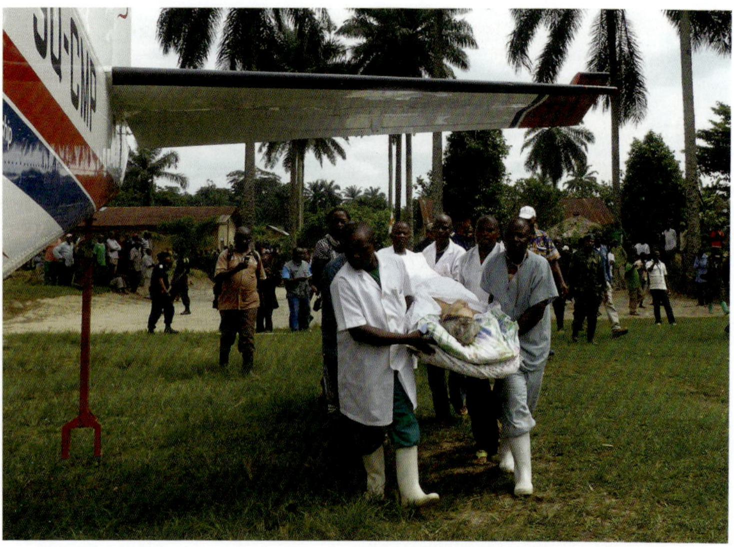

Maud air evacuation after shooting. Photo: J Cadd, MAF

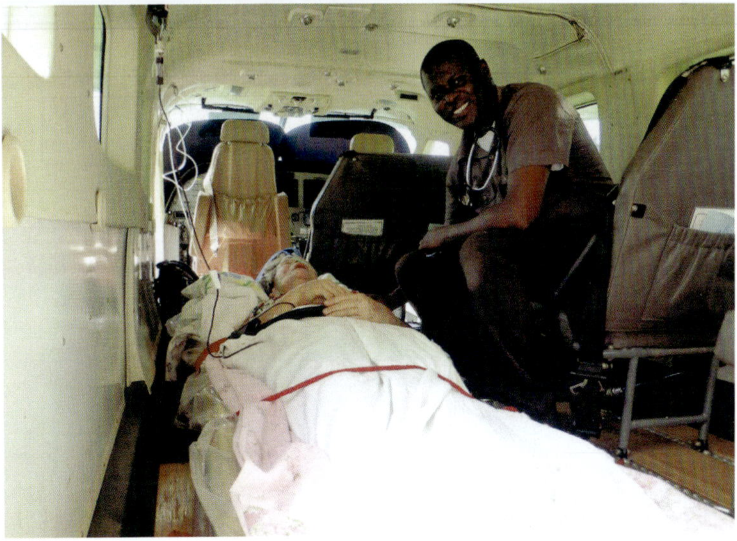

In the plane enroute to Nyankunde hospital after shooting, 2015

Presented with OBE, May 2015

Maud returns to Congo after recovering from shooting. Photo: J Cadd, MAF

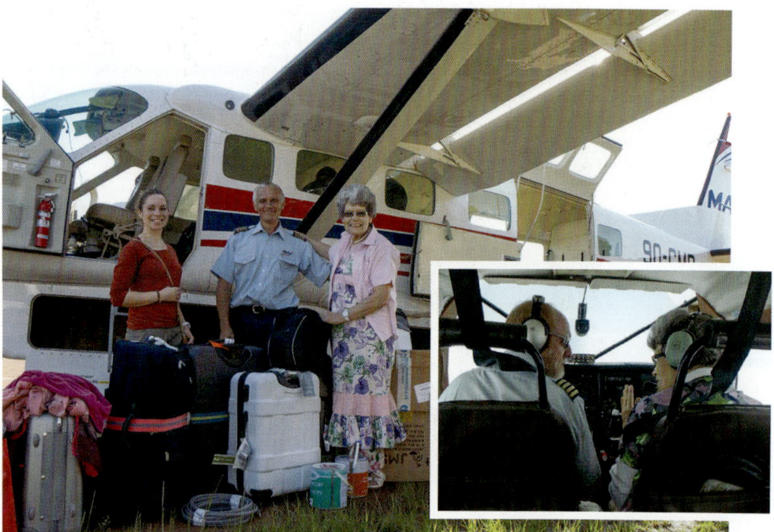

Elizabeth Craig, MAF pilot David Jacobson and Maud arriving at Mulita.
Photos: J Cadd, MAF

I had been on my own since my arrival in 1986 so it was a pleasant change but also an adjustment to have another missionary for company. With Roswitha's unusual personality and straight-talking manner, she made an interesting companion, and we enjoyed sharing meals, talking and praying together. As she worked in the leprosy camp during the day, we tended to meet at meal times.

Soon after her arrival someone came to the door with a baby chimpanzee whose mother had died. Feeling sorry for it, Roswitha adopted it as a pet, treating it like a baby and carrying it around, complete with nappy, in a locally made raffia bag. From this bag over her shoulder the baby chimp would pop its head out from time to time, giving us endless entertainment. It became very attached to Roswitha and was her constant companion all the time she was in Mulita.

For the first few months she shared my home but eventually, with help from the Leprosy Mission, we managed to repair Ida Grainger's old house so that Roswitha had her own space. We also needed to start building new brick houses for the leprosy patients as many of their little mud huts were falling down. I prayed constantly that the Lord would give our workers a heart and mind to work. There was so much to do.

Political unrest and corruption meant that roads continued to deteriorate. The economy had taken a dive, with inflation out of control. People were having difficulty obtaining enough money for essentials such as soap and salt. Every six months I would go to Kisangani to shop for hospital supplies. I looked forward to this trip as it gave me a break away from the usual situation in Mulita for three or four days. I stayed in the home of my Irish friend Maizie Smyth, who was based there with Unevangelized Fields Mission. She always had a bed ready for me and in Kisangani had the luxury of running water, electricity and a fridge.

On one of these trips Roswitha and I were almost stranded when we drove into a large hole filled with mud and water and hit a submerged rock. The protecting bar and steering damper on my Land Rover were badly damaged. We made it to Kisangani but I knew the return journey would be impossible. Fortunately Maizie was able to lend me her spare steering damper until I got back to Mulita to replace it. On our return trip we encountered four tin-mine trucks that had also broken down due to the woeful road conditions.

God seemed very real in the midst of disaster and I rejoiced in seeing Him deliver us in seemingly impossible circumstances. Sometimes, however, it was the succession of trivial difficulties that wore me out. The relentless calls upon my strength were more likely to wear me down than the dramatic crises that arose from time to time.

On one particular morning everything seemed to go wrong. The hospital was facing one problem after another, we were running out of drugs and two or three different situations arose at once all needing my attention. I came back to the house feeling exhausted, needing to sit down with a cool drink and take a break for a few minutes. However a crowd of people were waiting for me there. One person wanted books; another wanted a pair of glasses; someone had a sick child but no money; and a collection of people with complications and problems had gathered to talk to me. At 11.30 that morning I went into my bedroom and closed the door. Though it was only mid-morning, I was overwhelmed. 'Oh Lord, I can't take any more.' I sent a desperate prayer heavenwards.

'Hodi.' It was the usual greeting in place of a doorbell. I dragged myself to the door.

'*Mademoiselle*, can you help me please?' Large eyes looked at me in hope.

'I'm sorry, could you please come back in fifteen minutes? I just can't see you now.' I felt ready to explode. Returning to the bedroom, I took some deep breaths, called on the Lord for His help and steadied myself to face the demands of the rest of the day.

On another day there were so many people around my house, at the front door and the back, I felt as though I was being ambushed. I escaped to the only place where I could be sure of being alone: the outside toilet. For ten minutes I hid there, praying for God's grace, asking for His help and strength. Then I took a deep breath, came back to the house and began again. I needed that ten minutes' quietness. While I was in Mulita, I often felt there was no rest night or day, seven days a week, because I was constantly on call in the hospital, at home or out with the Land Rover for medical work. The daily demands of life that made me go and hide in the toilet threatened to overwhelm me.

But God provided a way out. While I had first been in Mulita with Ida Grainger, she and I had travelled to the village of Tschamaka, thirty kilometres beyond Punia. We had stayed with local Christians in Tschamaka while we held meetings and did outreach from the WEC church there. Ida had also introduced me to the staff of a large tin mine where Jim and Ida took their vehicle for servicing.

The running of the mine had been handed over to an educated African couple from Kinshasa just before I arrived. When I met the director, he was keen to help in any way possible. They owned a number of Land Rovers which they maintained at the mine and had all the spare parts I might need. A constant stream of lorries transported their tin to Kisangani and brought back supplies for the mine. They were happy to bring back building supplies for me on their return trips.

Although my initial reason for going to Tschamaka was their mechanical help with the Land Rover and other machines, I discovered an oasis where people cared for me and offered facilities I did not have at Mulita. I took my Land Rover and stayed for a week in their beautiful guest house while they serviced the vehicle without charge. I enjoyed their hospitality, had time to write letters which I could hardly get time for in Mulita, watched films and relaxed. I came back completely refreshed. It was God's provision for me, giving me new strength for the work at hand.

It was a great help having Roswitha, with her specialised training, to take over the leprosy side of the work. Her friendship as well as her help in the Bible school and church work encouraged me and lifted my spirits. Together with Dr John Harris she travelled round the leprosy centres in the province, with the help of MAF, researching the needs and planning a programme for the future of leprosy work in the area. Government medical inspectors approved her plans and encouraged her to pursue the work in outlying districts as well as Mulita hospital. Plans for a brick leprosy ward were under way although brick making was slow.

Idey's help also came just at the right time, with the opening of the new building and the expansion of the maternity work. In the Bible school Ikabu co-ordinated the teaching programme and planned to build more mud houses to accommodate extra students from outlying parishes. I was amazed at God's timing in all this help, as I was confined to bed on three occasions with recurring malaria over the course of three months. I was very aware that I could not carry the workload alone. God knew I needed a supportive team around me.

As the political and economic situation in Zaire deteriorated, the Zairois people could not contain their frustration. In September 1991 they reacted violently in the large towns and cities, looting, shooting and destroying shopping centres and markets. All expatriates, including missionaries, were advised to leave the country. It was the last thing Roswitha and I wanted to hear. Roswitha was in the middle of a new project for the leprosy work. We had stripped the roof off a ward to reroof it and were also reroofing the operating theatre; we did not want to be evacuated in the midst of all these projects.

The other frustration came from knowing there was no actual fighting in our area. Most of the trouble was in Kinshasa, the capital. But the British Embassy were insisting on all British citizens leaving Congo. Belgian and French paratroopers had come to Zaire to help with the evacuation. On the radio transmitter our field leader understood our reluctance but was adamant: 'You have to go. There's a plane coming to pick you up in an hour's time. The Wycliffe missionaries at Lubutu say the situation is very tense and you all need to get out now.'

We were not convinced. Lubutu was over 100 kilometres from Mulita. With one hour's warning, there was no time to do anything in terms of packing up or handing over work.

The MAF pilot had difficulty landing because of a difficult crosswind on the airstrip and was anxious about taking off again. We watched him walk up the airstrip and knew he was praying. We boarded the plane in silence, stunned by the suddenness of developments. We had no idea where we were going; we just knew we were being evacuated with no preparation and were concerned about the situations we were leaving behind.

Eventually we landed in Bukavu, on the Congolese border with Rwanda, high up in the mountains overlooking Lake Kivu. It was a beautiful setting, but the place was packed with Rwandan refugees and expatriates, including missionaries, all leaving the country. Most of them went off in cars over the border, leaving five of us behind in Bukavu. Reluctant to go, Roswitha and I stayed on, monitoring events day by day.

After about ten days, the situation seemed to be improving. President Mobutu appointed a new prime minister from the opposition party, which pleased the people. Life was becoming more normal and the violence settling. The MAF pilots had all left, but two ladies from the Borean mission who had remained knew some helicopter pilots still in a mission near Bukavu. The Borean ladies, in a similar situation to us, arranged for the helicopter pilots to fly them back to their mission station to complete an official hand over.

Inspired by their determination, I persuaded them to give me the pilots' radio transmitter number before they left and with some trepidation managed to contact them. 'We are friends of the ladies from the Borean mission and in a similar situation. Would you be willing to take us back to Mulita so that we can hand over our work to those staying behind?'

'Yes, we could do that, but we have no idea where Mulita is.'

I knew little about navigating from the air but thought quickly. 'If you can find the River Lowa, which runs into the main Congo River, I think I should be able to guide you. Mulita is not too far from the river.' I sounded more confident than I felt.

As we prepared to set off in the helicopter, my thoughts were running ahead: 'I'll never be able to do it. How will

I find a little settlement like Mulita in the middle of all that jungle? Lord, help me have wisdom and insight for this trip. Guide us to the right place.'

With my eyes glued to the view below, we flew north-west. True to his word, the pilot found the River Lowa, and I did my best to pick out landmarks from the air. Suddenly I recognised the tin mine at Tschamaka. As we followed the river south from the tin mine, the thatched and tin roofs of Mulita came into view. We found the airstrip and landed to the consternation of the local population. They could not understand this 'plane' that dropped straight down out of the sky with a propellor on top. Never having seen a helicopter before, the sight of Roswitha and myself emerging from it left everyone in amazement. It was a source of great conversation for weeks to come.

We were relieved to be back to pick up all the loose ends we had left behind, but knew we would probably have to leave again soon because of continuing unrest in Kinshasa. We carried on with our various projects and teaching programmes. However alongside that our priority was to prepare the team in Mulita for our departure. I managed to get the roof of the operating room almost completed and the kiln of bricks burned. I also finished teaching five students so that they could return to their health centres at Lubutu and Lowa as hospital and maternity assistants.

The next crisis was not long in coming. President Mobutu dismissed his new prime minster and chose another. This sparked off a violent reaction of more looting and shooting by soldiers and civilians. The foreign embassies began broadcasting strong appeals to all expatriates to leave Zaire without delay. Every day on the radio, before the BBC world news, came the message: 'Would all British citizens still living in Zaire please leave the country immediately.' Then followed a list of places where troops or aeroplanes would be available. When the Belgian and French paratroopers announced they were withdrawing their forces, our field leader would relent no longer; we had to evacuate completely. We could no longer ignore the crisis. We were not surprised but still reluctant to go.

It was difficult to explain to those outside the situation how hard it was to leave mid-term in the midst of all our construction and teaching projects. We had recently appointed new heads of departments in the church and medical work who needed guidance, training and supervision. The new head nurse proved to be unfaithful with the medicines which I left at Mulita when I went to Bukavu, so on my return I delegated their distribution to another nurse. Unfortunately he fell and broke his right arm on the day before we were evacuated for the second time.

As we prepared to leave, I had to place the whole situation in God's hands. At least He had enabled us to stay on for a month to finish projects and hand over most of the work in an orderly fashion. An MAF plane came in from Burundi to collect us and take us out to Bujumbura, where we caught flights back home. We left with heavy hearts and questions about the future.

11

CHALLENGES

Six months later, with the local situation stabilised, we returned to Mulita. I was encouraged to find the church, Bible school and medical work all going well. The building programme was continuing, although the economic situation was making materials like corrugated iron and nails difficult to obtain. The need for a brick operating theatre and surgical ward was urgent. My architect friend John Anderson designed and sent out a plan, and the work began.

In the meantime our reputation was growing and we began to have important visitors coming to see what was happening. The governor of Maneima province arrived with his entourage, including radio and television reporters. My house was the natural place for them all to stay overnight, but sleep was an impossibility as I watched the coming and going of soldiers, security people and journalists.

The following day, having inspected all we were doing, the governor congratulated us on our achievements and promised his help in the future. True to his word, having experienced the Lubutu–Mulita road, he arranged for it to be repaired, which was a source of great rejoicing. However once the visitors had gone, I made a decision and informed the construction team, 'I'm not going through that again. We're going to build a guest house.' So another building project was added to the list.

The end of June marked the end of another Bible-school year. The final-year students received their diplomas and were sent out as evangelists into churches in the surrounding areas. In June 1993 our director, Ikabu, went to direct the Bible school in Isiro. His wife, Idey, had almost lost her life in Mulita with the difficult birth of their fourth child. A short time before they left they received the tragic news that their three-year-old daughter had died in Ibambi with her grandparents. It added another dimension to our sorrow at their departure.

On New Year's Day 1994 our local chief performed the official opening of the new surgical ward. This was celebrated with great enthusiasm as workers re-enacted their particular jobs for the benefit of the gathered crowds and we all shared in the feast afterwards. It was a great relief to have a more hygienic environment for our surgical patients.

The economy of the country continued to deteriorate as roads became impassable, schools closed and many businesses went bankrupt. Reports were coming in of atrocities in neighbouring Rwanda, with a number of refugees finding their way across the border into Zaire. Because of the ongoing political and economic crises in Zaire, we were unable to obtain vaccines to prevent infectious childhood illnesses. Ongoing measles and dysentery epidemics claimed many lives.

Mama Betissa became very ill with dysentery. Just when we thought we had lost her, she began to recover. However one case after another spread through the compound, with many patients dying. My carpenter, Aloys, lost his son and daughter to the disease, then his only grandson, before succumbing himself. The lady who helped me in the house lost her only son at one year old. Not one family escaped – the hand of death touched each one in turn. I found it physically and emotionally draining, losing so many who were dear to me and identifying with the families in their loss.

Hygiene was a major issue. We set up an isolation ward for dysentery patients and had water and soap available at every entrance and exit around the compound. We built a succession of outside toilets. Every day I made up jerry cans of rehydration solution from filtered water, sugar and salt. Despite our best efforts, the disease continued to spread and people continued to die. The wife of our new Bible-school director succumbed and lay at death's door in the hospital. When I went to see her, she knew she did not have long to live but her faith was strong. She looked up at me and quoted Ecclesiastes 7:1: 'A good name is better than fine perfume, and the day of death better than the day of birth.' She knew she was going to be with her Lord.

For over a year the epidemic raged. Every time we thought we had it under control, new patients came in from the forest and it started up again. Eventually the doctors in Nebobongo suggested a different medication from the one we were using. It was the answer we needed. People began to recover, cases became less frequent and the crisis was over. It left every family devastated, mourning the loss of those who had gone, but relieved that the main danger had passed.

One night I went to bed very tired and praying for a good night's sleep. At 2.00 a.m. I was awakened for an emergency in maternity. The patient was a pregnant seventeen year old, an only child who had travelled with her mother for two and a half days, covering a distance of around 130 kilometres to get to our hospital at Mulita. They had walked through the forest, travelled sixty kilometres by canoe up the Congo River and were transported on bicycles the last eight kilometres, arriving at Mulita at 1.30 a.m.

As well as being very tired, Fatima was having strong contractions and was in obstructed labour. I did not know if she could stand a caesarean section after the journey she had made. We prayed and operated. At 3.00 a.m. we delivered a lovely baby girl and Fatima remained stable. The following day, when she realised all that had happened, she was filled with gratitude to God for His deliverance. She turned to Him, accepting Him as her Saviour. My tiredness was transformed into new strength as I watched the joy on that young mother's face replace the fear she had when she arrived. Despite all the challenges and frustrations, God was still at work.

In July 1995 Roswitha had to return to Germany as her mother was ill. When her condition improved, Roswitha returned to Zaire, but instead of coming back to Mulita, she began a leprosy programme in another province. Her departure left me once more the only missionary based in Mulita. My working day was busier than ever and I had a stream of visitors: students, both medical and tourist, seemed to find their way to my door; visiting doctors came to help with surgery; and other missionaries came to deliver seminars to the church. When three newly qualified nurses arrived on completion of their training, it was a much-appreciated help in the hospital, pharmacy and laboratory.

In January 1996 a new church president was elected. Rev. Kibuka was a gracious and godly man. At around forty years old he was relatively young to become president of the church but he was intelligent and spiritually mature. We were conscious of his need for wisdom to lead the church in the difficult days facing Zaire. The whole infrastructure seemed to be collapsing; education, medical services, communications and roads were all disintegrating.

Because of the collapsed economy and its consequences, soldiers were no longer receiving their salaries, so they began to harass the local population for money. On two occasions some of our workmen were stripped of their clothes, tied up and lashed with whips for trivial offences, all in order to obtain money. On both occasions I had to intervene. The soldiers accepted my objections with bad grace but released the men.

During one tropical storm a nurse's wife and four children were killed by lightning in a nearby village. Many believed it was caused by witchcraft. Tension grew throughout the day; villagers accused those they suspected of being responsible. That night we heard a commotion as trouble broke out between the local population and the police. Soldiers who came as backup added to the problem, attacking defenceless villagers. Surrounding villages were evacuated as the inhabitants went into hiding in the forest. This gave the soldiers opportunity to go through the empty villages looting and shooting.

On the heels of this incident, over Easter 1996, we had a visit from an eye surgeon, Dr Uketi, which we had advertised on the local radio. As a result hundreds of patients came from all over the area. The pilot who brought him had a surprise for me: 'I brought you a crate of Coca-Cola. You can give me the empty bottles when I come back for Dr Uketi.' I had not seen a Coca-Cola bottle for about two years so I was delighted.

Dr Uketi unpacked his equipment in preparation for the next day and we separated patients who needed surgery from those needing treatment. That night and throughout the next day trouble continued as local people and the army attacked each other, though we had no understanding of the extent of the unrest or that war was beginning throughout Zaire. Meanwhile Dr Uketi was working his way through hundreds of operations. I finished my ward round in maternity and went to see him in theatre as he was finishing an operation.

He looked hot and tired. 'Would you like a Coca-Cola?' I offered.

He gave me a grateful smile. 'If you can bring it before I start the next operation, that would be great.'

I ran back to the house, gathered up a bottle of Coca-Cola, some ice cubes and a glass, hopped on to my bicycle and raced back through the hospital compound to the operating theatre. Unfortunately at that moment Rambo, my Alsatian dog, decided to chase a goat right in front of my bicycle. Coca-Cola, glass and all went flying as I hit the ground.

Everyone came running to help. '*Mademoiselle*, are you all right? Let us help you.'

'No, I'm fine. I'll get up in a minute.' I gasped in pain as I put my hand to the ground. Crowds of patients and their relatives had gathered to watch.

'Maybe you could just help me stand up.' I gave in as I realised I could not put any weight on my hand. I had broken my lower right arm.

Dr Uketi stopped in the middle of his operations to set my arm and put it in plaster. I was embarrassed to be the cause of extra work in the midst of an already long operating list but tried to carry on hosting the surgical team as best I could with my arm in plaster.

Dr Uketi finished his operations and the team left on the plane the next day, somewhat to my relief. Meanwhile the local situation was becoming tenser. That evening a large group of soldiers arrived in Mulita, making their way along the road between my house and the village. They were escorting a group of people and carrying a variety of objects: sewing machines, bicycles, radios, pots and pans – everything they could manage. The clerk of works, in charge of our workers, had moved from the neighbouring village into our mission station because of what was happening.

'What is going on?' I asked him.

'Oh, the soldiers have arrested those people. They have looted the villages and are taking all they have found to their base in Yumbi. They are just passing through Mulita.'

I was indignant at the local people being treated in this way. Brandishing my plastered arm, I marched up to a soldier who was guarding some of the people. 'These people are very poor. They can't afford to lose all that stuff. It's not right to steal their belongings.'

He looked at me and said, 'Don't talk to me. Go and see him,' indicating the army commander.

I went over to the commander and repeated, 'This is not right, taking their possessions; these people are very poor.'

He replied, '*Mademoiselle*, you don't know but these are very bad people.'

'No, they're not,' I protested. 'I know them. This man here beside me, Samweli, he is a good man. He helps me and is very reliable.'

'No, no, he is the worst of them all. You don't know him.'

I insisted, 'I have worked with him for many years and he has been very faithful and very good to me.'

'*Mademoiselle*, you have no idea. These are very bad people.'

On his signal the soldiers started shooting in the air, putting an end to the conversation. I thought I had better be quiet at that point so I retreated as they disappeared with both people and possessions. The situation remained tense for the next few weeks, and many people remained in the safety of the forest. I reported the situation to Punia but the army there were involved in the looting. Not content to let it rest, I reported it to Kindu, the provincial capital.

Finally I had a response. At the end of May the governor sent his assistant together with the army colonel from Kindu. The assistant governor called the community together and asked people to come back from the forest to work in their gardens. He emphasised that they wanted peace, not fighting, in the area. He went to Punia to reassure the population there that all was well. Gradually people began to return to their empty houses. Their possessions would never be recovered but they began to pick up their lives again.

With my arm in plaster, I had not been able to make my regular trip to Punia to get hospital supplies. As the time approached for me to go on leave, I decided I needed to get to Punia, plaster or not. We needed barrels of petrol, paraffin oil for the lamps, sacks of salt and sugar, and various other supplies for the hospital. The plane was due to collect me a week later for my journey back to Ireland.

I set out in the Land Rover, driving as best I could with the plaster on my arm. Halfway to Punia, coming down a hill, one of my Zairian passengers said, '*Mademoiselle*, go slow. The bridge is no longer any good.'

It had always been a good bridge, but I took him at his word and put my foot on the brake. There was no response. I pumped at the brakes to no avail. I shouted, 'There are no brakes.'

'*Mademoiselle*, slow down.' Now my passengers were shouting too.

There was nothing I could do. The Land Rover speeded downhill towards the bridge. In a complete shock reaction I closed my eyes and took my hands off the steering wheel with an inner cry, 'Lord, get us over this bridge.' There were two logs crossing that deep river, on either side of the vehicle. Somehow when I opened my eyes, we were on the other river bank. Never in my life will I forget the sensation. I had done nothing; only the Lord had got us over that bridge. With one voice, everyone in the Land Rover said, '*Asante Mungu*' – 'Thank you, Lord.' No one could believe what had happened. To this day they talk about that miracle of deliverance.

Shaken by the experience, I completed the journey with great caution, using first gear on the hills as we had no brakes. Eventually we reached Punia and I did my shopping, picking up all we needed, as well as gathering up more passengers for the return trip. I was almost ready to leave when the officials from Kindu, having moved from Mulita to Punia to address the local population, spotted me in the Land Rover and waved me over. '*Mademoiselle*, come and join us on the platform.'

They were making a gesture of friendship in an effort to impress their audience.

I could not refuse but tried to plead my case. 'I'm sorry, I have to go. You know the state of that road and my Land Rover's not good. I've no brakes. I need to go early; I can't stay any longer.'

But they insisted, '*Un moment, Mademoiselle, un moment*. It will soon be over.'

I joined them before eventually convincing them that I had to leave. They brought their speeches to an end and took me off for a Coca-Cola before I started home. By this time it was growing dark.

Crossing the first bridge, we started up a steep hill, the Land Rover struggling under its heavy load. It was the darkest night imaginable – not a moon in the sky, not a star to be seen. Suddenly the Land Rover plunged into a big hole in the road where it jammed. I tried four-wheel drive but to no avail. I tried reverse; that was no better. I discovered that not one of us had thought to bring a torch. We could not move and did not have a light between us. I asked one of the passengers, 'Go and try to find us a light somewhere.'

A couple of people disappeared into the darkness while we continued trying to get the Land Rover out of the hole. It was about two kilometres to the nearest village. After some time they arrived back with a little local light, just palm oil and a wick, which fluttered in the darkness and was of limited help.

When pushing the Land Rover proved unsuccessful, we began to dig, changing the shape of the hole. Eventually the passengers managed to push me backwards out of it. I knew there was a precipice on one side of the steep hill but in the darkness I could not see where I was going. With myself the only one in the Land Rover and everyone else pushing, it began to roll back down the hill, gathering momentum without any brakes. Unable to stop, I was yelling in the Land Rover, 'Lord, help me get out of reverse. Lord, help me get into first gear.' As I crashed into first gear, off I went, up the hill, straight into the hole again.

For the next two hours we continued to dig. One of the passengers went to the nearest local evangelist about five kilometres away and obtained a hurricane lamp which was some help. Finally they managed to get the Land Rover out and we started on the way home. We had not gone half a kilometre when the engine died. We looked under the bonnet but everything appeared to be as it should be.

At the end of my tether, I said, 'We'll have to spend the night here because we can't go any further.' Two of the passengers, the leprosy nurse and the hospital secretary, offered, 'We'll go on to Mulita to tell them what has happened.' They headed off on foot while the rest of us spent the remaining hours of darkness in the Land Rover.

Daybreak came and it started to rain, the green of the forest veiled in grey. Two men from Mulita appeared with my bicycle, a solution which had not occurred to me. I sent a man to the tin mine at Tschamaka, requesting a mechanic to come and repair the Land Rover. Leaving a responsible helper in charge of it until the mechanic came, I set off to cycle back to Mulita.

Crossing the wet log bridge on the way back was not so easy with a bicycle. One of my helpers went over first, balancing with the bicycle. Then he came back and took me by the hand, one step at a time, shuffling sideways across the slippery log.

The hospital secretary, who was with me on this journey, questioned me afterwards. '*Mademoiselle*, why are all these things happening to you? Look at these last few weeks – a broken arm, fighting at Mulita, the Land Rover breaking down. Why are all these things happening?'

I replied, 'I have no idea, but I have proved the Lord in ways I have never had to prove Him before. I know that God is sovereign, in control, helping me through it. It has been great to know God's presence in it all.'

I continued packing up and preparing to go on leave. Meanwhile the mechanic and the local Roman Catholic priest discovered the timing belt in the Land Rover had snapped, so they replaced it and drove the Land Rover back to Mulita.

I asked, 'How did you get over that dreadful log bridge?'

'Oh, with great difficulty.'

I pictured again those two logs and how the Lord got the Land Rover balanced on them when I could do nothing. The vehicle arrived back the day before I left.

I knew the country was in a precarious situation. With rumours of war rumbling in the background, one of the messages God gave me to share with the Mulita church before I left was 2 Chronicles 7:14: 'If my people, who are called by my name, will humble themselves and pray … then I will hear from heaven, and I will forgive their sin and heal their land.'

12

THE LOST LAND ROVER

While I was in Ireland, Zaire featured on the international news, attacked from within and without. Together Rwandan and Ugandan armies invaded in an attempt to overthrow the government of Mobutu and take control of the country, launching the First Congo War in 1996. President Mobutu's thirty-two years in power had been years of steady decline. One of the world's richest countries in terms of natural resources, Zaire had become progressively poorer, with the whole infrastructure deteriorating to a fraction of what it had been.

The people rebelled against Mobutu and his government, destroying any remaining stability as foreign investors withdrew. Following the Rwandan Civil War between Hutu and Tutsi groups and the resulting genocide, Rwandan Hutu forces fled to eastern Zaire where they set up refugee camps. Together the Hutu militia and Zairian armed forces fought against Tutsis in Zaire.

Maizie Smyth, my UFM friend in Kisangani, returned from Zaire in November with disturbing news. Rebel soldiers, after looting and destroying Bukavu on the Rwandan border, headed west for Kisangani via Mulita. They looted the mission station and in particular the two missionary houses. They took everything including solar panels, car batteries, water barrels, medical supplies, books and household furniture, accumulated over many years. The Land Rover had also gone. I was concerned for the Christians in Mulita who were left devastated by these events.

Continued fighting between rebel and government troops made it impossible for me to return as planned in April 1997. The Simba rebels who had brought about such havoc in 1964 had reappeared under the name of Mai Mai. By this time they had taken over more than half of Zaire and appeared to be supported by the general population. Their leader was Laurent Kabila, a Congolese revolutionary and politician.

Communication with Zaire was difficult but I did receive one letter from the church president, Rev. Kibuka, in which he praised God for preserving his life when Isiro was taken over first by Zairian soldiers and then the rebels. He needed much wisdom to lead the church through these difficult days.

The areas where the Rwandan refugees were located suffered most as the refugees quickly devoured the little food which the local people had in their gardens. Widespread starvation resulted for both Zairians and Rwandans. Mulita was invaded by Hutu militia men from Rwanda as well as Rwandan refugees. Local resources were inadequate to cope with the influx, resulting in hunger and disease. People were reluctant to plant their gardens for the resulting crop to be plundered by refugees and soldiers.

In May 1997 Laurent Kabila was proclaimed the third president of Zaire when he took control of the country and ousted Mobutu. He changed the name of the country back to the Democratic Republic of the Congo, commonly referred to as DRC. The First Congo War culminated in the end of Mobutu's reign and the hope of better days under Kabila.

A semblance of peace and stability began to return and some of the churches started to communicate on their radios. However no one had heard anything from Mulita. Rev. Kibuka sent a message to Nairobi saying that my Land Rover was now being used by government troops in Kisangani.

In July Maizie Smyth and I decided to make an exploratory trip back to DRC. I planned to persuade government officials to return my Land Rover so that I could drive it down to Mulita with medicines and supplies for the hospital. Once on the ground, I would assess whether the roads were passable and our chances of making it through the many road blocks. If the journey was impossible, I would ask some of the Mulita leaders to come to Kisangani for talks and they could take some supplies back with them.

As soon as we arrived in Kisangani, one of the first things I spotted was my Land Rover. The best vehicle in the city, it was being used by government soldiers, who were filling it with petrol at the filling station. My immediate impulse was to go and ask them for the keys but local church leaders were aghast at such an idea. 'Oh no, *Mademoiselle*, you can't do that. You have to appeal through the proper channels.'

I followed their advice but it was galling to see it twice in the following two days as soldiers drove it around town. All my instincts were to march up to them, ask them why they had it and demand it back.

An interim government had been set up while war continued, so on our second day in the country I went to see the provincial president. Pastor Nonziadane, a former church president based in Kisangani, sent his personnel manager to accompany me. It was an ordeal to try and find the provincial president, squirrelled away in his office at the top of a five-storey hotel.

At the hotel entrance soldiers demanded to see my passport and other documents. Once everything was examined, we were frisked, reminding me of the Troubles in Northern Ireland. Security officials interrogated me about my background, my reason for being in the country, my desire to see the president. We were then allowed access to the first floor but there guards went through the same procedure. On each level we were searched and interrogated until we finally reached the fifth floor. After an hour of preliminaries, I achieved access to the man I needed to see.

He smiled and shook my hand. 'Good morning, *Mademoiselle.* How can I help you?' He was polite and well spoken.

'My Land Rover has been taken by government soldiers. I have seen it being driven around Kisangani. I need this vehicle to carry out my work and help people in your country. Can you arrange for it to be returned to me?'

'Of course. Peace and normality have returned to DRC. I understand the great work you missionaries do in the country and we want to work together with you. You should encourage other missionaries to return to the country. Let me help you.'

While I waited, he telephoned the army commander who had my Land Rover and asked him to meet me the following day to return it. The next day I went to the meeting place as agreed. After four hours' wait, it became obvious that the commander was not going to turn up. Frustrated and tired, we returned to see the provincial president, negotiating each floor of the hotel building as before, then waiting for another two hours to see him. Surprised that the commander had not appeared for our meeting, the president tried to telephone him again but this time was unable to reach him. Once more he proclaimed his desire to help and promised, with the governor's help, to recover my Land Rover during the weekend.

We returned to see him on Monday morning but there was still no trace of the Land Rover. He arranged an interview with the governor on the following day. On Tuesday I went back to the now familiar building with its prolonged procedure of accessing the fifth floor. This time the governor was there. Making the best of my opportunity, I recounted the whole story, before summarising, 'So you see, the commander didn't appear with the Land Rover as promised.' My face showed my frustration.

'Oh don't worry. I'll make a few phone calls ... Oh yes, there'll be no problem. You'll get it back.' He was very apologetic for all my trouble. 'You'll definitely have a response by tomorrow.'

With lessening hope, I climbed the stairs again the next day. The governor was polite but vague as to the whereabouts of the vehicle.

I was exasperated. 'But I've seen it a number of times being driven round the city by soldiers.'

'If you can find the Land Rover and inform me where it is, then I will authorise its return to you.'

We started a wide and fruitless search throughout Kisangani. Late in the afternoon the pastor in Lubutu, 300 kilometres from Kisangani, contacted us by radio to say the Land Rover was there being repaired by soldiers. The word on the street was that it was to be taken to Bukavu and on to Rwanda as one of their 'trophies of war'. I resigned myself to the fact that it was gone.

But I still wanted to get to Mulita. Many of the Rwandan refugees who had found their way there had settled on our airstrip, using it as their base. The MAF pilots, concerned about damage to the airstrip, were unwilling to risk landing on it until someone on the ground checked that it was safe. The only way to get back was to hire a vehicle and drive down from Kisangani. Maizie would stay in Kisangani but Pastor Siangombi, responsible for the churches in the southern area, had come from Mulita to help and would travel back with me. We also gathered up a number of passengers who wanted a lift south.

The next day, with the help of my church friends, I found a Land Cruiser which would transport us the 400 kilometres from Kisangani to Mulita, though at the outrageous price of 550 dollars. The door was held together with string and did not close properly. The radiator cap was the centre of an old maize cob. The fuel tank was a five-litre jerry can piped to the engine under the bonnet. Just to complete matters there was a leak in the oil tank so we had to stop regularly to top up the oil. Every so often the corn cob blew out of the radiator and I got a spray of boiling water round my legs. However I disregarded all these drawbacks and focused on my main goal: reaching Mulita.

Seventy kilometres of the Kisangani-to-Lubutu road were one continuous mud hole, through which we slipped and bumped as best we could. We spent the first night at a little Baptist church 112 kilometres from Kisangani. The area had been severely affected by the war and Rwandan refugees so people had only recently returned from hiding in the forest. We negotiated several army barriers and passed many broken-down tanks on the road. The following day we managed to cover almost 200 kilometres, arriving at Lubutu in the middle of a tropical storm.

I made a point of meeting the army commander without delay. 'I have been told my Land Rover is being used by soldiers here. Is this true?'

'Yes, it has been here. They have taken it to collect food on the Bukavu road. But now that you're here, we will return it to you as soon as they come back with the food.' He nodded to emphasise his point.

'I will probably be gone again by that time. The best thing is to return it to the church pastor here in Lubutu. He will look after it until I can get it myself.'

'We will do that. I will make sure the vehicle is returned to him.' He shook hands as if on a deal.

I thanked him and left. I did not hold out much hope.

After a night's rest we continued on the road to Mulita. Few vehicles were now using the road as it had disintegrated almost completely. As we entered each village, the cry went up, *'Mama Kells anarudi'* – 'Mama Kells is back.' We were surrounded by cheering crowds, but I found it hard to hold back tears as I looked at the joyful faces with emaciated bodies and ragged clothing.

We spent another night at a little mud church before finally arriving at the River Lowa. Instead of one day it had taken us three days to get there from Kisangani. We were now six kilometres from Mulita.

We heard that the Christians from several villages as well as Mulita had waited all day for me at the river crossing, complete with trumpets. They passed the time singing, knowing I was on my way. The diesel ferry which used to take vehicles across the river had broken down, overused by thousands of refugees in previous months. The only way across the crocodile-infested river was by canoe. Boarding the fragile craft with care, we paddled upstream close to the river bank, avoiding the fast-flowing current until we had gone far enough to launch out towards the far bank. We then allowed the current to carry us back to where the welcome procession was waiting. Their joy at my return seemed undimmed by the long wait for my appearance.

Together we walked the six kilometres to Mulita, trumpets playing, people singing and dancing as they went. As I looked back down the path, I felt like the pied piper with a line of people snaking behind us, the crowds growing with excitement as we walked. I had never received such a welcome before; I felt honoured and humbled. My return seemed to symbolise for them the end of the fighting and all the hardships they had endured; things were returning to normal. Certainly the difficult four-day journey from Kisangani was more than rewarded.

A stadium of banana trees and palm branches had been erected for the official welcome. Parades and speeches completed, we went into the church building to give thanks to God for His goodness in keeping us alive and reuniting us. Then followed an elaborate feast, prepared at cost by those who had lost everything. I heard many stories of God's protection during the war and the refugee invasion. I discovered the roof of the maternity department had been blown off in a tropical storm, ending up in the market place. A mud hospital ward had collapsed during a hurricane two weeks previously but miraculously no one was killed or badly injured.

I heard how the Christians had dug holes in the mud houses, including my hen house, to hide my things which remained after the looting in November. When we investigated, we found that in the damp conditions some of the hospital equipment was rusting and unusable; my clothes were so rotten they disintegrated in my hands. However a few items were recovered and I was grateful for the thoughtfulness of those who had tried to preserve what they could.

The hospital was completely out of medicines so the staff were delighted at the supply I had brought with me as well as basics such as soap, salt and paraffin oil for lamps. In the following days, over several cups of coffee and tea, I was regaled with accounts of exciting and sad experiences. The Rwandan refugees had camped on the airstrip until moved on by the soldiers. Refugee mothers had left their starving children with the Christians until aid workers from Save the Children and UNICEF came to collect them and take them back to Rwanda.

Then the questions came. 'How long can you stay? When are you coming back to live here? We need you here.' I assured them I would return as soon as possible.

I stayed for three days. Having inspected the airstrip, I decided it was fine for planes to land there. Wonderfully, the Christians had hidden the radio transmitter. When they produced it, I was able to contact the MAF pilots, who came and collected me. Promising to return with supplies, I flew north to Nyankunde, then on to Nairobi, from where I caught my return flight to Northern Ireland.

My plan was to replace all that had been lost in the war and return to Mulita with fresh supplies after one month. When I arrived home, however, I was unwell and my self-medication for malaria did not seem to be having any effect. As I was getting ready for church one Sunday morning, I looked in the mirror and realised my eyes were yellow. Because of my sun tan, I had not previously noticed the colouring on my skin, but now I suddenly realised I was jaundiced. I had probably contracted hepatitis from drinking contaminated water on that long journey down to Mulita. Normally I filtered and boiled all my water but that journey allowed no opportunity for such refinements. A week in the Royal Victoria Hospital saw me over the worst of the attack but it took much longer than that for my liver to recover. My promise to return immediately to Mulita could not be fulfilled, as disappointing to me as it was to the local folk waiting there.

While I was recuperating, I kept an anxious eye on DRC and especially the situation in Mulita. Rev. Kibuka paid them a visit and was a great spiritual blessing to the people. Dr Pat Nixon from Nyankunde was in the Maniema area to investigate medical needs and was able to bring some much-needed medicines. She arranged for further supplies to be sent to Punia on a regular basis where Mulita nurses could purchase them when required.

The economy of the country was lower than ever. With no money available for state salaries, people were poverty-stricken. Roads continued to deteriorate to the extent that my Land Rover, if ever returned, would be of limited value. In any case the story was that it had gone to Rwanda so it was unlikely that I would ever see it again.

WEC missionaries began to trickle back to their work in Isiro, Ibambi and Nebobongo. As my liver slowly returned to normal, I made plans to fly back to Mulita. Margaret Coleman, who had worked with her husband in the Mulita area twenty-five years earlier, asked if she could go back with me for a couple of months. Originally from Northern Ireland, she had been living in the south of England since her husband died but always had a desire to return to Mulita. Delighted to have not just a travelling companion but someone to support me in the work for a short time, I booked the flights.

My farewell service in Molesworth congregation was an opportunity to express appreciation to all those who had supported me during my time at home and who would continue to pray as I returned to DRC. I would be facing not just physical challenges but a spiritual battle. Dr Helen Roseveare spoke at the service, using the words of Pharaoh's daughter to Miriam in Exodus 2:9: 'Take this child away and nurse him for me, and I will give you your wages' (ESV). She shared a powerful message on how God used Miriam to fulfil His purposes even though she did not know God's plan for the way ahead. I returned to DRC holding this encouragement in my heart. I would need it in the days to come.

13

THE WHITE COAT

I had chartered a plane to fly Margaret and myself from Nairobi to Kisangani, then persuaded Jim Strait, the AIM pilot, to take us and some of our luggage on to Mulita the same day. On landing on the Mulita airstrip, we received a rapturous welcome, but immediately discovered that the situation had changed since my visit a few months earlier. A drunken army commander came bustling into our welcome party, a frown on his face. 'What plane is this? Why are you flying in here without my permission?'

'I live here,' I volunteered. 'I've just come back from the UK with supplies for the hospital.' I indicated the piles of luggage.

'I have not been informed about this. No one can land here. I am impounding this plane.'

Having persuaded Jim to fly us into Mulita, I was embarrassed that he was now being put in this position.

Over the next two hours we talked with the commander, trying to persuade him to change his mind. Eventually Jim, looking at the sky, remarked, 'I think I am going to have to stay the night anyway. It's getting too dark to fly back now.'

'Okay,' said the commander, suddenly relenting. 'You can go.'

Jim did not give him time to reconsider. Hopping into the plane, he started the engine and accelerated down the runway. I watched the plane rise into the sky with a prayer of thanksgiving to God for His intervention and turned to go to my house. However I was waylaid by a nurse calling me to the hospital. '*Mademoiselle*, can you come? We need help.'

'What is it? I haven't even got home yet.'

'I know but this mother cannot deliver her baby. She needs a forceps delivery.'

The local midwives were reluctant to use forceps so, following the nurse along the path, I rolled up my sleeves and prepared for action. I was delighted to arrive in time to save another life.

Once finished in the hospital, I made my way home through the compound. Tired after the journey and the stresses of the afternoon, I was ready to sit down and unwind with a cup of tea. To my dismay I discovered all the luggage in my front garden surrounded by armed soldiers. 'What's going on?'

'You need to open everything so that we can inspect it. We have to make sure you have no weapons hidden here.'

Realising there was only one way to resolve the situation, I complied. Once they were satisfied that I was not a threat, the soldiers left us searching for lamps so that we could see to move everything into the house. I missed the lights I had had before the solar panels and batteries were all stolen.

The situation was a shock to Margaret. At the age of seventy-seven, this was not the return to Mulita she had envisaged. The next day, Sunday, the intoxicated army commander turned up again. He stood at the back door of our house with another soldier, gun in hand, demanding to use our radio.

'You can't use it just now. We are leaving for church. The radio won't work with a dead battery anyway and an arrangement needs to be made with someone at the other end. It's time for us to go to church now.' I put him off as well as I could.

Muttering threats, he stomped off. When we came out of church, he seemed to have disappeared. We enjoyed Sunday lunch and a quiet afternoon. That evening I walked down the airstrip with friends as I usually did on a Sunday to check how work on it was progressing. Our hearts sank as the commander appeared but to our surprise he appeared calm and even friendly. 'What's going on?' I asked some of the other soldiers after he had gone.

'He was on drink and drugs this morning and came back to get ammunition for his gun when you wouldn't let him use the radio. We had to lock him in the house till the effects wore off. He was going to shoot you.' The soldiers were under his command but appeared to be prepared to exert their independence when they thought it necessary.

To my horror I discovered that soldiers were living on hospital premises and the commander had taken up residence in our guest house. After the arrival of our plane, they closed the airstrip, leaving the closest airport thirty-three difficult kilometres away, on the Mulita side of Punia.

The main road from Lowa through Mulita separated my garden and house from the airstrip. The commander erected a barrier on the road at the end of the airstrip, right in front of my house. Anyone who did not realise they were supposed to stop their bicycle at the barrier suffered the consequences. Several times a day we watched innocent people being flogged for some infringement of his rules. The commander would lift them up like a sack of potatoes over his shoulder and throw them to the ground. I had never witnessed such brutality or felt so helpless. The soldiers took over the isolation ward and used it along with the small brick toilets as a prison for their captives.

One night the commander picked out two prisoners, a man and a woman, claiming they were witch doctors. He had them beaten in the prison until the elderly lady died. Dragging the semi-conscious man out to the airstrip in the middle of the night, he had him shot. Within a few weeks five other people were accused of being witch doctors and were also killed by the soldiers, their bodies left to rot by the river or in the forest.

In the midst of all this trauma Margaret and I tried to carry on with normal life. The commander was constantly in my house, looking for coffee, food or something else. I tried to agree to his requests when possible, not wanting to alienate him further. One day he ambled into the living room and sat down opposite Margaret, the AK47 on his knee casually pointing straight at her. Terrified that it would go off accidentally, she demanded, 'Get that gun away from me.' Amused, he adjusted the gun's position, but it did little to help us relax.

Along with the local chiefs, we put in a complaint to the army headquarters in Punia. When nothing happened, we complained to the governor and to the various officials in Kindu, the provincial capital. A delegation came to investigate the allegations, which were backed up by the local population. The commander was removed and sent with his soldiers to the front line, where he was eventually killed. To our relief a different group of soldiers from Punia, more humane in their approach, replaced them in Mulita.

Our next task was to get back control of the hospital buildings. We complained at length to the authorities, who understood how important it was for us to have use of our buildings. The chief mobilised the population to build two long mud houses for the soldiers so they could move out of the hospital. Unfortunately the new houses were right opposite my house on the edge of the airstrip.

Despite the difficulties of our situation, Margaret rose to the occasion. It was reassuring to have her company and wonderful for us to be able to pray and trust God together for His solution. She helped in the Bible school, taking over my lectures, which gave me more time in the hospital. She was delighted to find she remembered her Swahili, despite the length of time since she had used it. Terrified as she was of the commander, she loved the local people and did all she could for them during the two months she was there.

It took me three weeks to get my house back into order but the hospital buildings were a greater task. They had not been repaired since I left in June 1996, so the leaf roofs were leaking and some mud walls collapsing. Much of the hospital furniture and equipment had been stolen, and most of the bedding had been lost or destroyed while hidden underground. With no beds, the patients had to lie on hard boards. It would take time to replace all that had been lost. Repairing and replacing existing buildings was difficult now that the roads were almost impassable, but all these seemingly impossible situations gave us opportunities of proving God in new ways and seeing Him answer prayer.

As Margaret's time in Mulita came to an end, we faced the dilemma of getting her out. With the theft of the Land Rover, I had no vehicle, and she could not walk or cycle the thirty-three kilometres to Punia airstrip. The week before she was due to leave, I set off on my bicycle to see if I could organise something. I arrived at the airstrip in time to see the MAF plane which had just landed with medicines for us and personnel for the British aid organisation Medical Emergency Relief International (MERLIN). MERLIN staff were working on a short-term relief programme in Punia and had a good vehicle. I cycled up to them, dust clinging to my sweating face. 'Hello, I've just come from Mulita. I'm trying to find transport for my friend to get here from Mulita next week. She needs to get a plane for the first leg of her journey back to England because she can't cycle that distance.'

The aid workers looked me up and down and decided I needed help. 'That's not a problem. We can come and collect her.'

'That's so good of you. Could I ask you to bring all these containers of medicine when you come?' I indicated the boxes awaiting transport to the hospital. It took many helpers to transport them by bicycle.

'Sure. We might as well make the journey worthwhile.'

I set off to cycle back to Mulita, thanking God for His guidance in Margaret's travel arrangements. I arrived home thankful also for the strength He had given me to cycle the round trip in one day.

I saw Margaret off in June and missed her cheerful company when she had gone. There was much to be done repairing houses, and sorting out problems in the hospital and church. We had made bricks before I left in 1996 but the building of the medical paediatric ward had not begun. I was ready to start the building project again in August when it was time for our annual WEC missionary conference.

On a rainy day I cycled with two local church leaders to Punia airport to fly to Isiro for the conference. The plane collecting us was also bringing medicines and books from Nyankunde, so sixteen workers came with us to transport the supplies back to Mulita by bicycle. We arrived at midday, but as the afternoon wore on, it became obvious that there would be no flight that day. It was too late to return to Mulita before dark so we decided to spend the night at the local church.

Next morning our hospital secretary arrived from Mulita. 'I have a message for you. The pilot was not able to contact you yesterday because of a problem with their system. He managed to get through on the radio to Mulita. He tried to fly to Punia three times yesterday but could not make it. He had to turn back each time because of bad weather.'

'Well, I can understand that.' I had been through similar situations enough times to trust the pilots to make a wise decision. 'Are they coming today?'

'No, they have other flights that must go ahead this week. He can't pick you up until Friday.'

It was now Tuesday. There was nothing else for it: I had to cycle back to Mulita, this time battling hot sun rather than heavy rain. Some of the others stayed to wait for the plane. However I wanted to finish up a few more things in Mulita and talk to the pilot on the radio transmitter there, our only means of communication.

Oblivious to the rising tensions outside our secluded area, my greatest concern when I woke early on Friday morning was how I was going to get to the airport. Claps of thunder competed with a continuous deluge of rain resounding off my tin roof. Lightening flashed, wind battered the house and streams of water flowed through the garden. I contacted MAF on the radio transmitter and described the conditions. 'I don't know if you'll be able to make it today. There is a tropical storm raging here – thunder, lightning and floods.'

The pilot was reassuring. 'Looking at our weather equipment here, the storm should be over by about 11.00 a.m. Go to the airstrip anyway and we will do our best to get there.'

I headed out into the storm on my bicycle. Four hours later I arrived at the airstrip just as the plane was landing. Soaked to the skin and covered in mud, I had to have a complete change of clothes before I could get on the plane. I climbed aboard, exhausted after my fight with the elements but grateful for dry surroundings.

In Isiro missionaries were gathering for the conference. The church president, Rev. Kibuka, left us for important church meetings in Kinshasa, taking with him a number of passports, including mine, to get residency visas renewed. Because of his relationship with the immigration authorities, it was easier for him to obtain permanent residency visas. That evening we were shocked to hear that another rebellion was starting in Eastern Congo and near the capital west of Kinshasa. War had been declared again and all the borders were closed. We spent many hours talking on the radio and listening to conflicting news reports. It became obvious that we had to leave the country as soon as possible.

I was dismayed at the prospect. I had left Mulita on a bicycle, to go to a missionary conference, expecting to be back in a week. Everything of importance was still in Mulita. Things of sentimental value, such as photographs of my early days in Congo, had been left behind, not even put away for safe keeping. I kept thinking of things I would have brought with me if I had realised what was going to happen.

War continued to spread and because many of us did not have our passports we were unable to obtain exit visas. In any case all the airports were closed. MAF had evacuated but we were communicating with their base in Nairobi by radio transmitter. They agreed to send a plane if we could get permission for it to land. Despite many attempts over the next two weeks, we were unable to obtain the required permission from immigration officials or the state administrator. Finally the head of the ANC, the Congolese National Army, told our church vice-president, Pastor Abule, 'Hide your missionaries'.

We had a difficult conversation with the pilots in Nairobi. 'We have tried over and over again but we can't get permission for a plane to land. What can we do?'

'We can't leave you there. We'll come and get you anyway but you'll have to go to Nebobongo because the airstrip in Isiro has been mined. Be in Nebobongo on Sunday morning at 10.30 with a small bag, ten kilos maximum each. If it's safe to land, spread a white sheet on the ground as a signal to the pilots. We will send two planes.'

Nineteen missionaries, from Wycliffe and WEC, piled into an assortment of vehicles to travel the seventy kilometres of rough road to Nebobongo. Many road barricades and the lack of road passes slowed us down. Reports came through that the rebels had taken Bunia and Nyankunde and were heading in our direction.

In Nebobongo a hostile crowd gathered as we assembled at the airstrip with our baggage. They began to berate us, shouting accusations at us: 'You're cowards running away from us. You're disobeying the government. You're the enemy.'

Before we arrived they had rolled barrels on to the airstrip to prevent a plane landing. In the midst of the commotion, the Congolese headmaster of the missionary secondary school in Ibambi appeared and quietly encouraged us: 'You are doing the right thing. Don't listen to those people. You need to go ahead and leave while you can.' We appreciated his wisdom and loyalty.

The men in our group managed to roll the barrels off the airstrip. At 10.30 we were all in place. As 10.40 approached, our eyes lifted to the sky, but there was no plane to be seen. We waited. 11.00 a.m. came and went. So did 11.15, 11.30, 11.45. We stood silently on one side of the airstrip, tense and nervous, the crowd jeering on the other. An hour after the arranged time, we were beginning to wonder if the planes would get through. By this time we were gathered in groups of two and three, praying for the Lord's deliverance. At two minutes to 12.00 we thought we heard the sound of an engine and all eyes were on the sky once more. Sure enough, there were two planes.

Our instructions had been clear: 'As soon as those planes land, don't hesitate. Jump on as quickly as you can.' We grabbed our luggage and, despite the heat, I put on my white jacket to make it quicker to board. We spread two white sheets on the ground as we had been instructed. Immediately the crowd ran on to the airstrip and pulled the sheets away. One missionary, braver than the rest of us, stepped forward and shouted at the top of her voice, 'In the name of Jesus, I command you to leave that sheet alone.' Four missionary children, realising what was happening, were screaming by this time. The rest of us were in tears. All we could think of was the 1964 rebellion. We were sure we were about to be taken hostage by the crowd. As the pilots saw the sheets being removed, they assumed it was too dangerous to land and turned their planes around to leave.

All of a sudden one of the Wycliffe missionaries yelled at me, 'Maud, give us your white coat.'

Realising what he meant, I pulled off my white jacket and threw it on the ground. As one of the pilots caught sight of it, he signalled to the other pilot. Together they turned back and came into land. With the engines still running, the co-pilot was at the door, pulling us on board, packing us into the aircraft. We were still fastening our seat belts as we took off, breathless with relief, unable to speak. It had taken only seven minutes for both planes to land, board nineteen of us and take off again.

An hour and a half later we were over Ugandan airspace. The pilot, Jim Strait, turned round and said to us, 'You can relax now. We're out of danger.'

He explained the delay: 'We started out on time but the rebels managed to access our frequency on the radio transmitter and warned us that if we tried to rescue missionaries, they would bomb the plane and take the missionaries hostage. We decided it was too much of a risk to continue. Meanwhile American satellite surveillance showed the rebels getting closer to Nebobongo and their advice was to turn back for you. We knew if we didn't get you out immediately, we never would.'

We could hardly take in our narrow escape. We wept tears of relief and were full of gratitude to the pilots who had risked their lives to save us.

At the same time we could not forget the accusations hurled at us at the airstrip. It was a sad and difficult departure from Congo. I recalled the Lord's word to me that morning: 'Then they cried out to the LORD in their trouble, and he brought them out of their distress' (Psalm 107:28). As relief at my safety and despair for Congo jostled for priority, I tried to rest in the knowledge that He who had brought us out of our distress could still the storm in Congo also.

In Uganda we landed at Entebbe to refuel. Across the tarmac came one of the Wycliffe missionaries, carrying my white jacket. I greeted it with amazement. 'How did you get time to lift that?'

'Oh, as I was getting on the plane, I tripped over it, so I just grabbed it. You might as well have it.'

I looked at the coat that God had used to save our lives. I would keep it always as a visual reminder of His delivering power.

14

A DIFFERENT DOOR

Stories of continuing conflict from DRC made a quick return to the country unlikely. Attacks from Rwanda and Uganda, supporting the rebels, had started the Second Congo War. This was followed by Angolan, Zimbabwean and Namibian armies entering on the side of the government. Ultimately nine African countries became involved.

There was little news from Mulita, although we did hear that the pastors stranded with me at Isiro at the time of our evacuation in July managed to cycle south and arrive home in time for Christmas. Other church leaders, including Rev. Kibuka, remained cut off in Kinshasa. Meanwhile, in Ireland, I was kept busy with requests to speak at meetings. In an effort to catch up with modern technology, I also began attending computer classes. I eventually received two letters from Mulita, reporting widespread looting. While some Christians were standing firm, others were losing their way spiritually. My heart went out to this little group of people, largely unknown to the outside world but precious to God.

At this time the Kosovo crisis was at its height. My friend Ed Morrow, who used to work in Nyankunde with UFM, contacted me about the possibility of going to Kosovo for a few months while I waited to go back to DRC. He was now working with Samaritan's Purse and looking for people to help in relief work there. WEC agreed that I should be seconded to Samaritan's Purse. However just as I was about to go, the war in Kosovo came to an end and the need for extra personnel became less pressing.

The focus of Samaritan's Purse had shifted to South Sudan, where war between the Arabs in the north and Christians in the south had been raging for the past sixteen years. The idea of going to Sudan attracted me because it bordered DRC and I would be able to monitor the situation from there. Initially I would go for six weeks, after which the situation would be reviewed.

In July 1999 I flew to Nairobi where I met up with Joel, a young American also going to work in Sudan with Samaritan's Purse. Joel and I waited in the terminal for the AIM pilot who would take us on the final leg of our journey into Sudan.

'Maud, what are you doing here?' The pilot grinned and stuck out his hand.

'Jim Strait! It's you again! We'll have to stop bumping into each other like this.'

Jim laughed as he bent to help us with our luggage and ushered us out on to the tarmac. 'I thought I wasn't going to get out of Mulita when the commander impounded the plane that time. And I've already evacuated you twice. It's getting to be a habit. That white-coat incident was a bit of a close call!' He stowed our luggage and helped us aboard the Cessna Caravan.

As he went through pre-flight checks and we settled into our seats, I could see him smiling to himself. Preliminaries completed, and waiting to take off, he looked over his shoulder at me and shook his head. 'I can't believe I'm flying you back into another war zone.'

'Oh, you know me. Can't keep away from trouble,' I quipped.

Samaritan's Purse had decided to reopen an abandoned hospital at Akot as a primary healthcare centre to cater for the needs of people returning to their home area. As these individuals and families straggled in, mostly from refugee camps in Ethiopia, various organisations such as Tearfund and Food Aid were helping with practical needs of housing, clothes and food. Samaritan's Purse had asked me to head up medical provision in the health centre. There had been no fighting or bombing in that area for some time, so it was considered relatively safe.

We arrived in Akot on Friday evening, settling into little individual mud huts in a big compound. In the centre was a communal hut for cooking and eating. The next day I spent unpacking and sorting out my luggage and supplies. I met Samuel, our Sudanese translator, along with the head nurse, midwife, pharmacist and auxiliary nurse who would be my colleagues in the hospital. Joel was in charge of logistics.

On Sunday Samuel came to me. 'Would you like to see the hospital before starting work tomorrow?'

'Yes, that's a good idea. I'd love to do that.' I was eager to get a feel for the situation.

We set off in the pickup along the narrow road to the hospital building, two kilometres from the house. Suddenly he drew the vehicle in under a tree.

I was puzzled. 'Why are we stopping here?'

'Do you not hear those planes overhead?'

'Yes, I do hear a plane but I didn't think anything of it.'

'Those are Russian Antenov planes. The Northern Sudanese are coming to drop bombs.'

I had a sudden insight into what it must be like for Sudanese to be attacked by their own people, North against South, Muslim against Christian. Our Christian hospital was a target.

A couple of minutes later we heard the bombs being dropped and a thump as they exploded. We sat where we were for half an hour, afraid to move until someone came along.

'Where did the bombs fall?' was our first question.

'In the bush, behind the hospital.'

It was just where we planned to start work the next day. When we eventually summoned up the courage to go closer, we discovered five bombs dropped around the edge of the compound. Large craters and pieces of shrapnel marked where they had fallen. None of our buildings were damaged which was a miracle. Nonetheless we had to report the incident to Samaritan's Purse leaders in Nairobi, who immediately wanted to evacuate us by plane the next day.

I refused point blank. 'I've only been here three days; there's no way I'm going to be evacuated. I'm staying where I am.'

We praised God for His protection and started work on Monday morning as planned. The hospital consisted of a series of small cement-block buildings with tin roofs. We repaired five of these to use for outpatients, a pharmacy, maternity, an inpatients ward and a laboratory.

My job was to oversee the work of the health centre, set up pharmacy controls and supervise the equipping of the centre. It was wonderful to see how the Lord provided our every need. We co-ordinated with Roger, Ed and Bethany in the Samaritan's Purse base in Nairobi, reporting back there and ordering necessary supplies.

I was delighted to care for the sick who needed help so desperately, but it was difficult to treat so many as outpatients who should have been inpatients. The referral hospital at Billing, where the very ill patients were supposed to go, was a difficult three-hour drive from Akot. With ours the only available vehicle, we had to drive them there. The mud-hut hospital did not have good reports of recovery so many of the patients refused to go.

I had the opportunity to share God's word every morning at our 'devotions' for staff and patients and also at church most Sundays. Church was held in the open under a Lulu tree. In that parched area, too dry for palm trees, the spreading Lulu was vital for its nuts and oil as well as the shade it provided for meetings. The Anglican church building had been bombed and rebuilt so many times that they had decided not to build again. As I did not speak the Dinka language, either the pharmacist or head nurse translated my simple gospel message. This eventually began to bear fruit as people became interested in the gospel and I was able to purchase some Dinka cassette tapes for them in Nairobi. The radio operator and some of the patients put their trust in Christ.

During my third week I was asked to provide cover at Lui hospital, which was bigger than the centre at Akot, as the expatriate staff who worked there were going to Nairobi and other places for Christmas and New Year. A Samaritan's Purse plane flew us from Akot to the closest airstrip, about ten kilometres from Lui hospital. On landing we met the staff from the hospital who were waiting to leave on our plane. They gave me some instructions for the handover of the work. Concentrating on what I was being told, I paid no attention to what was happening with the luggage. The pilot unloaded what he had brought for the hospital and loaded the luggage for the outgoing missionaries.

I did not look for my personal luggage until I arrived at Lui. As we unloaded all the medical supplies and groceries, I suddenly realised that my suitcase was not among them. I had arrived in an isolated spot with not even a handbag.

I had packed my passport, toiletries and everything else together in one case, deciding that it would be easier to transport one piece of luggage and I would be at less risk of losing anything.

Eventually I managed to get the pilot on the radio transmitter. 'I can't find my suitcase. Do you have it?'

'Yes,' he said. 'It's here. It came to Nairobi with all the other luggage.'

I was relieved to have traced it but knew it was too much to ask for a return flight just for my suitcase. I would have to wait till the plane came back again to be reunited with my luggage.

So there I was in the hot Sudanese bush with nothing: no change of clothes, no toothbrush, no Bible, no money to buy anything. It reminded me of Jesus sending out the disciples when He told them, 'Take nothing for the journey – no staff, no bag, no bread, no money, no extra shirt' (Luke 9:3).

But I had to survive for the next two weeks. The staff at the hospital provided meals so I would not starve. In a store room I noticed some old Samaritan's Purse tee shirts and lengths of navy cloth patterned with white ships. When I got to the hospital, I realised the cloth was for bedcovers. I decided to use this cloth as a wraparound skirt to wear with the tee shirts while I washed my own clothes. Each night I washed out my underwear and hoped it would be dry by the morning. Samaritan's Purse had English Bibles for the patients, English being the national language in Sudan. I came across a few toothbrushes and toothpaste which were there for patients. From the office I procured pen and paper. Gradually I managed to accumulate a survival kit to carry me through the next two weeks.

I was more concerned about my passport than anything else. It was essential to have it with us at all times in case we needed to leave the country in a hurry. So I was very relieved when the plane returned for me and I was reunited with my luggage and passport before flying back to Akot.

I celebrated the new millennium with my Sudanese friends in Akot, the local chief and his entourage, the army commander and his entourage as well as Samaritan's Purse workers. They killed a bullock for the occasion. At the feast, on 1 January 2000, I had the opportunity to share God's word with over 100 guests.

With so little in the way of help and supplies, I was constantly cast on God for wisdom in my work in the hospital. During the rainy season many children were brought in with convulsions caused by high fevers, malaria and other illnesses. Tuberculosis was widespread. On three different occasions adult patients were carried in who were paralysed from the waist down. Each proved to have TB of the spine and responded well to treatment. How we praised God when on discharge from hospital they were able to walk home.

On another occasion we received five patients with grenade wounds. I was planning to transfer them to the hospital at Billing when Dr Marcus Muller, a missionary from DRC, arrived. He was lecturing elsewhere in the country and needed to use the airstrip in Akot. 'There's no other airstrip available,' he explained. 'This is the only place we could land.'

'Do you have time to look at some patients for me?' I asked. 'It would be better than taking them to Billing.' I was keen to make the most of the opportunity.

'I have two hours to spare. Let's have a look at them.'

He had just enough time to treat the wounded patients. I was delighted to see how God was making 'all things work together for good' (Romans 8:28, ESV).

One outstanding miracle during that time was a little two-year-old girl who was burned from head to foot, back and front, after falling into a fire. We nursed her outside under a mosquito net, where she lay on a blanket and plastic sheet on the bare ground. We did not have enough sterile dressings to cover all her wounds daily so we just painted her with gentian violet. She was a wonderful little patient and drank her medication without any fuss. Miraculously she escaped the infectious diseases rampant in the centre at that time and in six weeks was completely healed. We stood back in awe at what God had done.

At that time the normal work pattern for Samaritan's Purse missionaries in Sudan was six weeks' work followed by one week out of the situation. Sometimes I did twelve weeks and then had two weeks off. On one of these longer breaks I went home to Ireland, where I spoke around the country about the Sudanese work I was now involved in. Teenage twin girls saved up their pocket money and bought footballs for the Sudanese children.

Arriving back in Sudan, I decided to take a photograph of a football game so that I could send it home for the girls and let them know how much their gift was appreciated. I was busy taking photographs when the ball came in my direction. Oblivious to the photographer, the children ran straight into me, knocking me over. As soon as I fell, I knew I had broken my wrist. With no medical help around, I pulled it straight and got it into line as best I could, before calling out, 'Joel, can you help me? I've broken my wrist.' I clutched it in place.

'Maud! This wasn't in my job description.' Joel was shocked.

'I need a splint. Can you find something?'

Joel recovered enough to find a length of wood and together we made a splint, binding the wrist in place as well as we could. Next he offered, 'Let me get you some pain killers. I'll contact Ed and Bethany and let them know.' He radioed Samaritan's Purse.

They sent a plane the next day so that I could go to Nairobi for X-rays and have our homemade splint replaced with a proper plaster. Then I returned to Akot to resume my duties, with a careful eye out for footballers. I was due to go home the following week in any case.

I arrived home from Sudan to distressing news about my sister Irene in Canada. The year before she had phoned me in Ireland with greetings on my sixtieth birthday. In the course of the phone call she had told me she had been diagnosed with bowel cancer. After eight months' chemotherapy and a holiday in Hawaii to convalesce, the cancer had returned in her lung and the prognosis was not encouraging. When I met up with Dr Helen Roseveare and her friend Dr Pat Morton, they told me, 'If you want to see your sister alive, go now.'

My older sister, Margaret, and I left immediately, with my arm still in plaster. We had two special weeks with Irene in Vancouver, sharing meals together and even going shopping. Before we left, she assured us she was at peace and was ready for God's will for her. Two weeks later she was gone, slipping peacefully away into the Lord's presence. She died in April 2000, exactly a year after her diagnosis.

In October 2000 I joined Wycliffe missionary Jill Brace on an exploratory trip back to DRC. We obtained visitors' visas and were permitted to take in medicines, books and other supplies. The first weekend we attended a women's conference at the Wycliffe base on the outskirts of Isiro. I then left Jill at her house and continued on to Nebobongo and Ibambi.

The local people welcomed me back with parades, singing, speeches and finally a feast at the head pastor's house. I was overwhelmed with emotion as we praised God together. The week seemed like one extended celebration as Dr Mola, the first Congolese doctor for Nebobongo, and Bernd, a German engineer, also arrived that week, each receiving an equally warm welcome. The church was packed to overflowing on Sunday for the main service, which lasted six hours and ended with us celebrating the Lord's Supper together.

All too soon the week ended. However back in Isiro I was delighted to spend some time with Rev. Kibuka. Stranded in Kinshasa during the war, he had experienced a very difficult time with his life frequently in danger. Eventually he had to fly to Kenya. Now back in DRC, he still had the missionaries' passports and permanent residency visas that he had been obtaining for us when we were evacuated. I explored with him the possibility of visiting Mulita in the spring of the following year.

Pastor Siangombi cycled 110 kilometres from Mulita to Lubutu to talk to me on the radio. It was wonderful to be brought up to date with all the news, good and bad. On a recent visit to Mulita the governor had been impressed with the work going on there so Pastor Siangombi had made a request for the Mulita airstrip to be reopened. We all prayed that this request would be granted.

Just as I was making plans to visit Mulita in January 2001, President Laurent Kabila was assassinated, plunging the country into uncertainty and making the visit impossible. Nonetheless I had established that the north of the country was relatively free from danger and the church leaders agreed I should prepare to return to DRC after completing my final six weeks in Sudan.

When I returned to Sudan, I prepared to hand over my work to two Kenyans. Just three weeks before I was due to leave, a UNICEF official informed us that around 1000 child soldiers would be demobilised from the front line and brought to Akot that weekend for rehabilitation into civilian society. They had to be evacuated immediately.

That evening two trucks brought the first child soldiers. Over the next two days several large UN world food programme planes delivered a total of 1705 boys between the ages of eight and fifteen years. The UN asked us to care for their medical needs – an enormous job as many were malnourished, and had high fevers, malaria, pneumonia and bad leg ulcers. I had repaired and redecorated an old building as a vaccination clinic so we were able to use it to treat the child soldiers.

One boy, Santino, arrived on the first flight with bad leg ulcers. I tried to distract him by chatting while I dealt with his painful legs. 'How did you get involved with the army, Santino?'

'Six years ago they forced us to join at gunpoint,' he replied. 'I was very young. After two or three years when the fighting was bad, I escaped and ran home. But my parents had both been killed and the rest of my family had disappeared. I had nowhere else to go. I had to return to the army.'

Many of the boys had similar stories to tell. Some of the younger ones were tearful and emotionally traumatised. We were stretched to the limits of our ability as we tried to deal with their complex needs.

When the leaders of Samaritan's Purse and American Southern Baptists in Nairobi heard about the child soldiers at Akot, they immediately mobilised help. A medical team was sent in to care for them. Food, clothing and emotional support systems were set up. Samaritan's Purse brought in equipment to show the *Jesus*[4] film and start Sunday schools.

It was difficult to leave Akot amid such a crisis but God makes no mistakes. As I boarded the plane home, I thanked Him for His perfect plan and for those who were taking up the challenge in Sudan.

15

REBUILDING MULITA

'Pastor Siangombi has been captured.' Rev. Kibuka was phoning from Kinshasa. 'He was trying to mediate between the rebels and the authorities. The rebels have taken him hostage along with others from the Mulita area. We don't know where they are.'

Recovering from my time in Sudan and preparing to go back to Congo, I was dismayed by this news. Pastor Siangombi, who fulfilled many roles in Mulita including Bible-school director and Bible translator, suffered from severe hypertension. I wondered how he would survive. Mai-Mai rebels, community-based militia groups, were still active throughout the country and this new action put my return to Mulita in question.

President Laurent Kabila had been succeeded by his son Joseph Kabila, who called for multilateral peace talks and agreed to share power with former rebels. In August 2002 the presidents of Congo, Rwanda and Uganda agreed to sign a peace agreement and we were hopeful that the war was coming to an end. Foreign troops began returning to their own countries and were being replaced by a UN peacekeeping force.

In September, however, serious inter-tribal fighting broke out in the Nyankunde area. Nyankunde Mission Hospital had been set up by five different mission boards in the 1960s and had an outstanding reputation thanks to the work of doctors such as Dr Becker and Dr Helen Roseveare. The large hospital, nurses' training school, medical centre, pharmacy and agricultural school at Nyankunde were all destroyed in the fighting. Hundreds of people were massacred, with patients killed in their beds. Missionaries were evacuated by air. Over the next two weeks thousands more were killed in the Nyankunde area.

Marion Baisley, a Brethren missionary who had refused to leave, walked through the destroyed maternity ward, heartbroken at the devastation around her. Suddenly she heard a weak cry. It seemed impossible there would be anyone left alive in the midst of the chaos. Following the sound, she came to a mother who had been shot dead where she lay. A young baby lay against her, trying to feed from his mother's breast. Gently Marion lifted the baby and carried him away from that scene of death and destruction. Joining others who were walking to safety, she trekked with him for nine days through the forest until they reached Oicha, an AIM mission station 150 kilometres away. There she passed him on to a Congolese family who agreed to care for this new little life until the situation settled and some family members could be found. They gave him the name Baraka Safari, meaning 'Blessed Journey'.

Many thousands were displaced. Not one building in Nyankunde was left with a roof. It underlined for us the temporary nature of buildings and material things. Only the spiritual work done in the hearts of the people remained.

We heard reports that since the war erupted in August 1998, up to two million people had died in north-eastern Congo. Many of the deaths were caused not by direct attacks but by malnutrition and lack of essential medical supplies. I was desperate to return to the country to bring in the needed medicines and do what I could to counteract some of the effects of the war.

In October I flew to Nairobi, then on to DRC in the company of some Wycliffe missionaries. WEC was naturally hesitant about the return of missionaries after the massacre in September. I was allowed back on two conditions: first, that I alternated six months in Ireland with six months in DRC; and second, that I took a satellite phone so that I could always be contacted. My nephew-in-law, Allan McKeown, Pamela's husband, kindly researched and obtained an Iridium satellite phone for me, connecting it up to my laptop. Hopeful of my new computer skills, I also planned to keep in touch through email. As there was no longer any bank or post office operational in the country, I carried all the money I would need for the next six months in cash.

In Nairobi I heard the good news that Pastor Siangombi had been released and that the rebels were leaving Mulita, making it safer for people to return from the forest. Arriving in Nebobongo a few days later, the only missionary back there, I was as delighted to see the people as they were to see me. We set up solar panels to charge the car batteries, which in turn powered the radio transmitter and satellite phone. This enabled me to contact pilots about flights, send home information about the situation in DRC and generally keep in touch with the outside world.

On my first Sunday there I was asked to speak in the church service. My heart was moved as I looked out over the congregation. 'We have lived through difficult days. We have seen war and rumours of war. But God has been with us and will be with us in the future. Jesus has promised He will come back again. We need to be ready when He comes.'

God's Holy Spirit touched hearts and forty-two people responded to the appeal to get right with Him. I thanked God for bringing me back and for His moving among the people. This was the reason I had come to Congo in the first place: to introduce people to the Saviour.

The following week brought me down from the heights of Sunday. In the hospital I was shocked to find the maternity postnatal ward full of infected patients, many of whom had had caesarean sections. When I started to do daily ward rounds, I discovered part of the reason to be lack of medicine, but it was also lack of hygiene. I gathered together a workforce of both relatives of patients who had no money to pay for their medical treatment and nursing students who could not pay their college fees. A clean-up operation got under way as they carried water, washed, scrubbed, painted, dug latrines and built two mud houses over the next five months.

On Christmas Day thousands of people gathered in Ibambi for a huge *makutano*. At the morning service outside I preached on the angels' announcement of Christ's birth. At the end Pastor Ikabu, leading the service, asked if anyone would like to get right with God. Young men began to come forward, which was unusual. As more joined them, the crowd at the front grew, many falling to the ground crying out to God for forgiveness of their sins. The Lord's presence was very real; even church leaders were confessing their sins and getting right with God.

One lady, who was heavily pregnant, rolled on the ground, calling out to God. I thought, 'She's going to hurt that baby' and was tempted to intervene.

'*Mademoiselle*, don't touch her,' Mama Damari laid her hand on my arm. She had lived through the Congo revival in the fifties. 'God's Holy Spirit is in control. He will look after her and the baby.'

The work of God lasted for hours, with more than 120 people responding. In the end Pastor Ikabu asked all who had come forward to come into the church building. Going from person to person, we counselled and prayed with each one, encouraging them to study the Bible and deepen their relationship with God – we knew it was easier to respond at an event than to persevere in living the Christian life. It was a remarkable and memorable day of blessing, as though God was reminding His people that He was still in control and had good things in store for them, despite all they had suffered. His Spirit was at work in a way we had not experienced before.

At the morning service on Boxing Day we again felt God's presence. Afterwards people dispersed to go back to their villages, with a new sincerity in their faith and a new determination to follow God in their daily lives. Some could not read and others had no Bible, but we encouraged them to meet together for Bible study and trusted God's Spirit to continue the work He had begun in their lives.

The following day I cycled to a distant village with two women helpers to run women's seminars. We encountered some soldiers on the road there and back, and over the next few days fear and unrest mounted. Soldiers were looting and shooting as they fled from a new group of rebels in Isiro. We were advised to hide as the fleeing soldiers came in our direction, but I felt God assure me of His protection and carried on with my usual routine. They passed my house and the hospital but stopped at the nearby market, demanding money, food, sponge mattresses and any means of transport they could find. Twenty kilometres up the road at Pawa hospital they forced the doctor at gunpoint to open the safe, then tied him up while they helped themselves to the cash.

Under the new group of rebels the local situation became more settled. Talks were being held in South Africa to try to bring an end to the war and draw up a new constitution for DRC. I was making plans to return to Mulita with Rev. Kibuka when the Mount Nyiragongo volcano erupted near Goma, directly on our way to Mulita. One hundred and forty seven people died and 400,000 fled from the city as lava destroyed all in its path. Most of the runways at Goma International Airport were covered, making it almost impossible to evacuate people or get outside aid to survivors.

With the door to Mulita closed once more, I turned my attention to what I could do in Nebobongo, dividing my time between the maternity department and building projects. Employment in the latter gave people some desperately needed income. Many were too poor to afford food or medical treatment and many ill people, especially children, were dying in their villages from treatable diseases. Many women remained at home to have their babies because they had no money to come to the hospital, but ended up with ruptured uteruses and dead babies as well as requiring hysterectomies. We prepared and planted three large gardens, providing food for the patients and a sense of fulfilment for those who worked there.

Throughout 2003 reports trickled in by letter and radio, informing me of the difficulties which the Mulita church was experiencing. Many buildings had been burned to the ground and those left standing had been stripped of their contents. Mai-Mai rebels were still active in the area and local people had fled into hiding in the surrounding forest. Those taken hostage had been released but some people were still too frightened to return to Mulita, including the Bible-school students. A large number of people had died, not just because of the fighting but also due to lack of food and medicine. I was desperate to return to Mulita.

Prayer was answered as the main rebel groups stopped fighting and agreed to join President Kabila in the new transitional government. Gradually the tribal rebels in the Bunia area and Mai-Mai rebels in the Mulita area also agreed to stop fighting.

In January 2004 the situation finally resolved sufficiently for my return. Rev. Kibuka, with his wife and youngest daughter, flew with me to Punia airport where we were met by a large delegation of church people. A local Muslim businessman, with the only available vehicle in the area, kindly transported us in his truck from the airport to Mulita. On the road the village people were out to greet us with singing and dancing.

At Mulita a large crowd had gathered for the official welcome. With no water barrels left in the village, children ran to the nearest waterhole half a kilometre away and brought me drinking water. Once I was ensconced in the seat of honour, the programme began. Singing, speeches and a re-enactment of the war helped to update me on events during my absence. Dressed like the Mai-Mai rebels in black and white, with replica guns made of wood and sticks, the men built a little hut and set it on fire. They acted out fighting each other and popped balloons as gunfire. I was touched by the preparation that had gone into the event. Welcome ceremonies were always important, but the warmth of their love on this occasion was all the more striking from people whose lives had been devastated.

The usual feast followed, food pressed upon me by smiling women. 'This food is so good,' I commented, savouring each mouthful. 'I don't know how you make it so delicious. I've missed this while I've been away. But where did you manage to get meat?' I looked out across the village. It was strange to be here with not an animal in sight. Everything had been eaten during the war.

The women laughed. 'The goat and chickens came from thirty-five kilometres away. We had to have meat to welcome you home.'

Finally I managed to see my house. I was grateful for the sponge mattress, bedding and eating utensils which

I had brought from Nebobongo because the house was bare. The only contents were some broken furniture and my old friends the rats who had taken over in my absence. I set up the new radio transmitter, antenna, satellite phone, solar panels and batteries to replace what had been stolen.

Government soldiers had been based in my house, with the Mai-Mai rebels in the operating theatre suite, just across from the Rwandans who were in the maternity unit. In the outpatients department and hospital wards the Rwandan-backed RCD (Rally for Congolese Democracy) soldiers, another rebel movement, had taken up residence. Many lives had been lost in the battles fought at Mulita.

After seeing me settled in, Rev. Kibuka and his family left to return to Isiro. As news spread that that I was there, people began to emerge from hiding in the forest where they had been living in leaf-roofed shelters. They came empty-handed. What the rebels and soldiers had not stolen, forest humidity and insects had destroyed. They had existed with little or no food to eat, unable to plant gardens and so searching for berries or insects that were edible. The Christians had tried to keep their Bibles intact but it was difficult in forest conditions. Their most immediate requests were for Bibles, reading glasses and medicine. People began to believe it was safe enough to build mud houses and plant gardens for food. Mulita began to feel like a village again.

Most mud buildings had been burned to the ground but the structure of the brick buildings was still sound. Carpenters and masons returned to help repair my house and furniture. I was able to purchase essential supplies, including the important rat poison, in Punia, and soon had my house habitable once more. As I cycled through the villages along the road to Punia, people shouted, 'Mama Kells is back. Mama Kells is back. The war is over.'

All the furniture and equipment had been stolen from the hospital and Bible school but the aid organisation MERLIN in Punia helped us out, providing medicines and some money for salaries. Gradually the hospital began to function again. Until my arrival the only light available at night had been from little palm-oil containers. Now we had the luxury of my solar-powered torch, which was especially helpful for doing caesarean sections at night.

The airstrip had not been used since war broke out in 1998 and had reverted to forest, with trees growing on the runway. A few days after my arrival the chief called in men from the surrounding villages. 'Now that *Mademoiselle* Kells is back we need to be able to use the airstrip. I want you to cut the long grass first and then cut down the trees.'

'Yes, planes need to be able to land here again. We will do it.'

The men were enthusiastic but with their limited tools it was a greater task than they anticipated. Many tree trunks needed to be removed and the holes filled in to make it level enough for a plane to land. Before it was completed, my six months were up and I had to leave, so I once more cycled the thirty-three kilometres to the airport. A delegation of church leaders from Mulita saw me off, promising that the airstrip would be ready for my return.

However six months later MAF pilots declared the airstrip not yet safe for use and landed in Punia, giving me detailed instructions about the work needed to make the airstrip useable. They unloaded all the luggage I had brought with me. Thinking I would be landing in Mulita, I had brought much: thirteen cartons of medicines, three solar panels, car batteries and other necessary supplies which I had purchased in Kampala, as well as all my personal luggage including the essential satellite phone and laptop. I surveyed it in dismay. How was I going to get it all to Mulita?

Just as the plane took off, the MERLIN pickup vehicle arrived to collect a passenger. The driver offered to transport me and half my luggage, leaving the rest of the luggage in Punia to collect later. Once back in Mulita, I unpacked and distributed the much-needed medicines to the hospital and health centres. We installed the solar panels and batteries for my satellite phone and laptop. A tour of the hospital, church and Bible-school buildings showed that many required reroofing. The question was where to start.

The nurses had the loudest voice so we started by rebuilding one nurse's house, then replacing roofs on others – some with leaves; the rest with corrugated tin. Despite lack of food and fear of the reappearance of the rebels, the Bible-school students gradually came back as they saw things beginning to return to normal.

One difference in the work was the decrease in the number of leprosy patients. In 1996, just before the war, a new treatment had been introduced which for the first time gave leprosy patients hope of a cure and a return to normal life. After the evacuation to the forest during the war, most leprosy patients did not return to the leprosy camp at the hospital. No longer contagious, their life was transformed and they were able to go back home to their villages.

On Sunday 14 November 2004 I joined Dr Helen Roseveare and Dr Pat Morton in Nebobongo, together with a number of other missionaries, the church president, a crowd of civic officials and as many others as could get within hearing distance. We had gathered for the official opening of a new surgical suite, named after Helen, in honour of the many years she had given at the hospital. Over the entrance was a wooden carving saying, 'Centre Chirurgical Mama Luka.' 'Mama Luka' was Helen's Congolese name, after Dr Luke in the New Testament. On her final visit to the country Helen had the joy of dedicating the operating suite, a valuable resource for years to come. Heavy rain did not deter the parades which were held outside, with thanksgiving for all that God had done and would continue to do in Nebobongo.

On our flight back to Punia the pilot collected some tin roofing for me and we arrived at Punia airport in time for me to cycle back to Mulita. Several Congolese friends transported the tin, five sheets at a time, by bicycle.

After Christmas and New Year work started in earnest again, teaching in the Bible school, preaching in church on Sundays and doing daily ward rounds and consultations. In between all this I was supervising the ongoing building work. Sawyers cut down trees and transformed them into planks; this required a full-time team of at least four, sometimes six, to keep up the necessary wood supplies. Carpenters, masons and brick-makers were all kept busy constructing a medical ward, an administration block and a doctor's house, as well as completing the airstrip. There were also numerous meetings to attend, problems to be solved and hospitality to be provided for the various visitors who came to help us.

We managed to complete the airstrip in time for the arrival of Bettina, a German Wycliffe missionary, and her team on 2 March. Bettina was working on the translation of the New Testament into the local language, Kikomo. A cheer erupted as the plane touched down on Mulita airstrip for the first time since April 1998. We had reached another milestone.

The following twelve days were full as I finished off projects, attended to the visitors and tried to pack up. On the day I left, Larry, the pilot, landed in Mulita with sixty sheets of tin roofing and four sacks of cement. Leaving the supplies for the Mulita workers to make use of in my absence, I boarded the plane along with Bettina and her team.

The highlight of my time at home in 2005 was Dr Helen Roseveare's eightieth birthday celebrations on 21 September, including the launch of her latest book, *Digging Ditches*.[5] Friends from WEC International and Girl Crusaders' Union gathered together with Helen for a meal. Her friend Rev. Dick Lucas, former rector of St Helen's Bishopsgate in London, sent a message congratulating her on being 'retyred'. Just ten days older than Helen, Dick said, 'Welcome to the Octogenarian's Club! There is only one rule – no retirement, because there is so much work to be done!' All of us there thanked God for what He had done through Helen over the years and for the blessing of knowing her as our friend.

16

REFINED BY FIRE

Flying in over Mulita in November 2005, I looked down over the little airstrip and the collection of buildings taking shape below, picking out my own house and the guest house. Nearby was the hospital and staff housing, the old leprosy camp off to the side, then the church and the Bible-school complex. My heart lifted as I thanked God for this place of His calling, for His people here and for His enabling for whatever lay ahead.

One of our priorities was to lay the foundations for the new paediatric ward. Groups of musicians from our Punia and Lowa churches approached me for work so that they could purchase musical instruments. Alongside making bricks for the paediatric ward, they helped us repair the almost impassable road to Mulita and prepare the ground for a new brick building for the primary school.

It was encouraging to have all this help but supervising all the workers, builders and airstrip-cutters ate into my time each day. I found it frustrating to be pulled in so many directions: caring for the hospital patients, doing pharmacy work and – of course my greatest joy – sharing God's word in church and Bible school.

One morning I was in the middle of a ward round in the maternity department when a man came running in. '*Mademoiselle*, come quickly, the kiln is on fire.'

I looked at him in bewilderment. 'What do you mean? It's supposed to be on fire.'

'No, no. The roof, everything is on fire.'

I followed him out of the hospital and realised that indeed the whole thing had gone up in a huge bonfire, flames leaping into the air as a crowd gathered to watch in disbelief. Soon the roof collapsed onto the bricks in a shower of sparks, sending the crowd running for cover. As the fire died down, we realised that every part of the kiln had disappeared apart from the bricks. They were well fired by the time the fire cooled seven days later and we were able to retrieve them. We had built the kiln too high for the leaf-roofed shelter, so the flames coming out the top of the kiln had set the roof on fire. We did have a metal-roofed kiln which was safer but had rejected it as being too far from our current building project. We learned our lesson.

The image of the burning kiln and the surviving bricks remained in my mind long after the event and became a symbol to me of my work in DRC. Many times I detected God's refining fire removing the rubbish – the earthly and unimportant things – furthering His purifying work in my life and the lives of our Christians at Mulita.

Over the years, especially during the war, almost everything I possessed was stolen or destroyed: my Land Rover, radio transmitter, solar panels, water barrels, bicycle and many other possessions which seemed important to me at the time. But God's word, which I had taught over the years, remained. Alone in the forest, as illness struck, as Christians turned away from God and as war erupted – putting me under threat or sweeping me out of the situation – I had my human moments of darkness. But God was in the fire. He brought me through, stronger in the end for having experienced it all with Him. What I suffered was mild compared to what some of the local Christians faced but His church in Congo remained, refined, purified and stronger for having proved Him in extreme situations.

Over the following months I saw God's refining fire at work many times. Our church president's wife took ill suddenly and died, leaving him to raise and educate their six children. Another evangelist lost his lovely young wife and child while she was giving birth in an outlying area. His brother lost three children from malaria within one year and yet another brother lost two children. A Bible-school student died of AIDS. Some of the Christians lost loved ones through illness and death, only to have their pagan relatives adding to their grief by taking all their possessions. Others lost properties through fires, for which they had to pay huge fines as well as losing everything.

Meanwhile workmen had to be dismissed and others, including our clerk of works, had to be disciplined for immorality. Our hospital administrator suddenly announced his resignation just as we were preparing to go to Nebobongo for the annual medical conference. My laptop crashed, leaving me without email facilities until I got back to Ireland. But throughout this refining process God remained my faithful, unchanging, solid Rock, steadfast and sure. I praised Him for the lesson of the burning kiln.

In February 2010 we finally completed the paediatric ward, ready for the official opening by Dr Sammy Kobinama and Chief Mangbukele, who came from Nebobongo for the ceremony. The Mulita area remained peaceful, allowing us to invite specialist consultants to treat and operate on needy patients. Dr Listro, a Congolese eye consultant, operated on nearly 100 patients during his week with us. Some of these people had walked long distances through the forest to receive surgery. It was wonderful to see the joy on the faces of previously blind patients when their dressings were removed following cataract operations and they could see again. Balancing this was the disappointment of other blind patients who had walked up to 300 kilometres to be told by Dr Listro that he could not help them. There was much blindness due to untreated glaucoma, which distressed us as well as the patients.

My aim was to get the primary school, Bible school and church completed in time for the WEC centenary celebrations in 2013, marking 100 years since C.T. Studd's first expedition. Over that time many had experienced the love of God transforming their lives; we had much to celebrate in the birth and growth of WEC International and the local church.[6]

However an ongoing malaria and anaemia epidemic in Mulita was causing many deaths – forty children in one week in August. The hospital ran out of medicines and MERLIN withdrew from the area, leaving our medical staff with no support. We prayed that these epidemics would be brought under control.

Back in Ireland I suffered an attack on a different front. On 25 September 2012 I returned home in the evening after speaking at a meeting in Belfast. Trees swayed in the wind as I made my way up the drive and parked my car in the garage. Opening the back door of the house, I felt a draught of air and saw letters ripped open and thrown on the floor. The contents of the hall cupboard were strewn across the floor. I could not even get into the bedroom because the mattress had been pulled off the bed, and cupboards and drawers had been emptied. In the living room cupboards and bookcase were also emptied onto the floor, but for some reason my laptop remained untouched. The front door stood ajar.

Stunned by the chaos, I telephoned my sister Margaret and then my neighbours. Margaret came immediately with her husband, Colin, and son, John. Unable to get through to the local police station, I phoned the emergency 999.

Two policewomen arrived and I stood in the hall of my home with all these people. Suddenly I was filled with the knowledge that God was in control. All the stress of the situation was replaced by an inner peace. My body was still full of nervous energy but in my heart I knew that God would work all things together for good.

The thieves had broken a bathroom window on the gable wall between my house and my neighbour, where it could not be seen from the road. They had obviously entered by the window and gone out through the front door.

My neighbour was keen to help. 'I'll nail up the bathroom window to make it secure for tonight.'

'I'm afraid not,' replied the police firmly. 'No one can touch anything until the forensic people come tomorrow.'

'But I need things from my bedroom for tonight,' I exclaimed. I was upset enough without being barred from my own bedroom.

'Sorry, we'll have to close off the bedroom. You can use the rest of the house.'

I spent the night in the spare room, next to the bathroom with the broken window. Although the bathroom door was locked, I lay sleepless, trying to take in what had happened. Suddenly I remembered the wallet containing my passport. People had given me gifts of money – some in euros, some in sterling, some of which I had changed to dollars. It was all in a special travel wallet, along with my vaccination certificate and my permanent residency visa for DRC, in my bedside cabinet. Another bigger wallet held money in an envelope which I was planning to bank the next day.

Unable to get into my bedroom in the morning, I could not rest until the police appeared at midday to answer my main question: 'Could you please look for my wallet and passport in the bedroom first?'

They searched the bedside cabinet, but there was no wallet to be seen. The forensic team were unable to find any prints; the thieves had obviously worn gloves and left no clues.

It was three weeks before I was due to go back to DRC. Flights were booked, medicines were ordered from Joint Medical Stores in Kampala and an MAF plane had been chartered to take me from Entebbe to Mulita. That afternoon I went to the post office and applied for a new passport. Telephoning the passport office, I explained how urgent it was. I had less than three weeks to organise a letter of invitation from DRC and all the documents needed for passport and admission into the country. Unable to go to the DRC Embassy in London in person at this stage, I found an agency online that would deal with it all on my behalf. God worked another miracle and the passport finally arrived the day before I was due to fly out.

In the meantime the local paper had picked up the story and the BBC arrived to interview me. People started sending gifts to replace what had been taken. In the end I had more cash to take to DRC than was stolen. But my permanent visa, stamped into my stolen passport, was gone, never to be replaced. From that point forward I would have the hassle of applying for temporary visas each time I entered the country. Also irreplaceable was old jewellery from my aunt and mother, but I was reminded again of the relative unimportance of material things. We need to hold them with open hands.

Although aware of God surrounding me with His care, I nonetheless found this intrusion into my personal space very traumatic. I installed an alarm, which gave me reassurance when returning home at night. In a new awareness of my vulnerability, it was one of the times when I felt God closest to me. It was good to know that He was in control whatever the situation.

I had just settled into the work in Mulita once more when we were sent orders by the government to close our airstrip because of rebel activity in the Goma area. Promises of protection from God's word made me conscious of His peace despite conflicting news of renewed fighting in Goma and surrounding areas. Tribal fighting broke out near us at the beginning of the new year, with mob violence terrorising the local community. The regional chief with his security officials called the opposing sides together and drew up a peace agreement.

However a few weeks later came the next attack. The Raia Mutomboki rebels were approaching Punia. Top of the list of people they wanted to execute was the state administrator. Hoping I would be able to get a plane to fly them out, this official arrived in Mulita with his wife, two children and their female house help. As soon as he stepped out of his pickup, a crowd armed with sticks and machetes descended on him. He fell to his knees and pleaded with them: 'Please do not harm me. I am doing you no harm. I just want to leave quietly. Please spare me.'

Horrified, I ushered the family into my house where they hid under the beds, shaking with fear and the women crying hysterically. Even as I was closing the window shutters, someone lashed out at my arm with a stick.

'We need to get out of here. Can you call a plane for us?' the administrator pleaded desperately.

'I'm sorry, I really want to help but I can't get a plane at a moment's notice. Your best way is to drive to the River Lowa and get a ferry across there on to the Lubutu road. You can stay here until it is safe to leave. We'll pray for God's protection.' I tried to speak calm into the situation, encouraging them to trust God to deliver them.

After some time things seemed to quieten down outside. As the excitement lessened, people began to lose interest and drift away. Deciding this was the time for them to make a run for it, I opened the door and encouraged the women and children into their vehicle. As the state administrator emerged, however, a roar went up and the crowd surged forward. With one arm around the state administrator's shoulders and the other protecting him from the front, I ran with him to the car and helped to shove him inside. With people running after the vehicle and jumping on the back, the driver took off and I dashed back to the house.

I was not the focus of their anger. With great relief I watched the crowd disperse as the vehicle left for Lubutu. The family seemed to appreciate my prayers for their protection as well as my practical help. I prayed that through this ordeal they would come to know God in a real way. I was to find out later that my name was also on the rebels' hit list.

Since 2009 we had had our own doctor in Mulita hospital. At this time, however, the situation in Punia and Mulita deteriorated so much that Dr Joseph and his family evacuated to Kisangani. Many of our local people built shelters in the forest, transporting their meagre possessions there. Only a few of us remained in the village, to stop looting as much as anything else.

We began to receive soldier patients with gunshot wounds, which was not a good sign. I tried to communicate this information to praying friends but could not get a satellite signal or contact anyone on the radio transmitter for three days, causing concern in Ireland and elsewhere. When I finally managed to get a signal, I received twenty-six concerned emails, including three from MAF saying they would evacuate me as soon as they heard from me. When Dr Matthias Holmer, a German missionary friend, heard me trying to make contact on the radio transmitter, he immediately answered and told me that MAF had a plane on standby to evacuate me; they thought I had been taken hostage.

I managed to get the necessary permission for the plane to land the following morning. After a sleepless night, I packed up the contents of my house and handed over the work. Once more I was evacuated, this time to Nebobongo hospital, where I spent the next few days in bed with malaria. Thankfully I recovered in time to join the WEC centenary prayer group.

Doctors Philip and Nancy Wood, the missionaries who had replaced Helen Roseveare in Nyankunde, had arranged the WEC centenary celebrations in 2013. As part of this initiative, anyone connected to WEC International was invited to tour some of the mission stations in DRC and see where the mission was founded 100 years before. We visited C.T. Studd's grave, his first church in Nala near Isiro and other significant spots, stopping to pray at each of them and taking it in turn to lead a devotional time for the local people.

I travelled back to the UK with some of the centenary prayer group and in September further centenary celebrations took place in Bulstrode. Various ministries within WEC International were represented with Helen Roseveare, at the age of eighty-eight, as the main speaker. As she and I travelled there from Ireland, we enjoyed the opportunity to thank God together for all He had done in the country to which He had called us.

The situation settled down in Mulita and I was able to return later in the month to help prepare for our local centenary celebrations. Dr Kibuka, now dean of the university in Bunia, was invited as our special guest. State officials were also present as the official opening of our seven-classroom primary school and administration block took place. Almost 400 children paraded in their new school uniforms and we celebrated with much singing and dancing. We rededicated the whole hospital complex to the Lord, ending with a thanksgiving service for His faithfulness over the years.

In October 2013 WEC leaders from around the world travelled to Isiro to share in the closing centenary celebrations. A parade attended by thousands of people marched into the stadium where they were addressed by WEC International directors, Drs Louis and Susan Sutton, various retired missionaries plus local church and civic dignitaries. In honour of the occasion the church presented an award, the *Brevet de Mérite*, to church president Modebali, his wife, Bettina, some elderly pastors and myself.

A few days before Christmas I was feeling unwell and had what I assumed was a painful infection in my right eye. Paracetamol and antibiotic treatment had no impact. When a rash eventually appeared across my forehead, I realised I had shingles. On Christmas Day I was supposed to speak at a huge *makutano* but had to spend the day in bed. I was studying the pharmacy book, wondering how I could access treatment for shingles, when a Congolese nurse friend called to see me. I explained my dilemma.

'I know that treatment,' he said. 'I have it in my office.'

I was sceptical. He travelled back to his office and reappeared the next morning with the exact pills I needed, together with special eye drops. He had been at a Heal Africa seminar where he was given free samples of aciclovir. The chances of anyone having the required medicine and of that person visiting me just when I needed it were so remote that I acknowledged God's miraculous hand at work once more. Within a few days I began to recover, the fever went down and I felt much better. Without the treatment I could have lost the sight of that eye.

In Mulita the newly built school was packed to overflowing, with up to 400 children attending. Unfortunately they brought their younger brothers and sisters with them, being responsible for them while their mothers were working in the forest. This was scarcely conducive to learning, so a nursery school was needed for the younger ones.

Having agreed on the best location for the nursery school, we prepared the ground and mobilised people to go to the river two kilometres away to carry back the necessary stones for foundations. The local tailor was employed to make uniforms. The last anthill on the Bible-school compound was used to make the bricks. At the beginning of 2015, with Christmas and New Year celebrations over, I hoped to get the nursery school finished before I went back to Ireland.

Of course I had no idea of the events that lay ahead that Sunday night when I went to bed as usual. But God, who had been with me since He first called me fifty years before, was still in control. When I went to sleep trusting in Him, my confidence was not misplaced.

17

AFTERMATH

As the mists cleared, I became conscious of hands cleaning me up, of faces hovering above me. I realised John, whom I had trained to take over from me in maternity, was erecting an intravenous drip to replace fluids. 'You're alright, *Mademoiselle*. We've stopped the bleeding and dressed the wound. You're on the couch in your house and I'm just putting up this drip for you.'

Behind John I could make out the nurse surgeons Nguza and Ramazone, attending to me rather than patients in the hospital.

'What are you doing here?' I asked. 'Go and see to that poor lady waiting for the section.'

'She's fine, *Mademoiselle*. Don't worry.' John tried to keep me calm.

The room seemed to be full. Local people had come to offer help and to see what was happening. Gradually I recalled the hoax call and the attack that I had thought was going to end my life. Perhaps my work in DRC was not yet finished.

The pastor sent some people to look for my attackers and others as messengers. They informed the chief of the area, who lived at the Lowa ferry crossing six kilometres away. At 3.00 a.m. the chief arrived with his entourage of soldiers and promised to contact his superiors in Punia, the army commander and the state administrator. Our resourceful hospital secretary lifted my camera from a nearby cupboard and began taking photographs of all that was happening, building up a photographic record of the night. Among them are pictures of the chief and police interviewing me in my semi-conscious state at 3.00 a.m.

I described the two men I had seen at the time of the attack, although for some reason the police thought there were three. They immediately despatched a search party and at 4.00 a.m. returned to tell us they had picked up one of the men trying to find his way out of Mulita. Not being from the area, he did not know the roads and had been found by local people, who brought him to the police.

A German company who were working on the roads in thc area agreed to lend the chief a vehicle to get to Punia. On the final leg of the journey he overtook the messengers whom the pastor in Mulita had sent by bicycle to the church leaders there, and so he gave them a lift into town. With the difficulties in travel and communication, it was 5.00 a.m. before the news of my shooting eventually got out beyond the local area.

Church leaders in Punia tried to contact the church president but his phone was out of order. However they managed to get through to Dr Mola, who had been our first Congolese doctor in WEC. He and I had established a firm friendship back in 2002 when we lived next door to each other for two years in Nebobongo. Dr Mola contacted everybody, including WEC headquarters in England and MAF in Nyankunde. My friends in both organisations were upset at the news but sprang into action. MAF immediately rearranged flight schedules so that a plane could come and pick me up.

In the meantime a rumour spread locally that I had died. The governor, afraid that the shooting might be the start of a major incident, sent a large number of troops from Punia, armed with guns and grenades. My death could have set off a spiral of violence. Thankfully God preserved my life and saved Mulita from any further trauma.

John monitored my vital signs, checking the dressings and keeping me reassured when I was conscious enough to hear him. He reminded me that everyone in the church was praying. Mama Jani, my faithful house help, washed my dress and cleaned up the mess in the house. When I asked her later how she managed to get the blood out of my dress, she replied, 'You always taught us to soak uniforms in salt and water overnight when there was blood on them so that's what I did.' Thoughtful and practical, she packed a bag in preparation for my transfer to hospital.

At midday everyone was relieved when plane engines were heard overhead. The MAF pilot was Jon Cadd, a good friend. He came with other good friends of mine, German missionaries Dr Matthias and Sabine Holmer, who were based at Nebobongo. As soon as they heard what had happened, they volunteered to come down and help with the evacuation. Jon was delayed first by bad weather at Nyankunde and then needed to fly to Nebobongo to collect Matthias and Sabine, so eventually reached Mulita twelve hours after the shooting. By then I was almost unaware of what was happening, though I had a vague sense of people coming into the house.

Jon, Matthias and Sabine brought medical equipment and blood donated by another missionary, Mareike from Germany. Over the next ninety minutes they gave me blood, did an ultrasound to assess the extent of the damage and supplemented my difficult breathing with oxygen. Preparing to take me to Goma where there were British troops with more medical equipment, they contacted the British embassy. However when their investigations showed that my lung damage did not appear to be as extensive as first feared and they managed to get my blood pressure raised to a more normal level, they decided they could do all they needed at Nyankunde hospital. I have no recollection of those ninety minutes of treatment, of being taken to the plane or of the two-and-a-half-hour flight to Nyankunde, but by the time I got there I was beginning to regain consciousness.

I came round as we landed roughly on the uneven terrain at Nyankunde, aware that kind hands were moving me from one place to another, taking me from the plane and transporting me to hospital. Still largely oblivious of my surroundings and with no sense of time, I experienced a great sense of relief to know others were taking care of everything.

The Mulita hospital staff had sutured the back wound and put in a surgical drain. At Nyankunde they opened the wound to check if there were any remnants of bullet. Once satisfied that it was clear, they sutured it again. However it refused to heal, so five days later they removed the sutures and left the wound open with drains in place, continuing to dress it two or three times every day.

Dr Kibuka's wife, Alua, and my friend Sabine both stayed with me throughout the first night in hospital. The next night Mama Alua stayed alone with me and was most solicitous. Every time I moved in bed, she said, '*Mademoiselle*, are you OK?'

'Yes, I'm fine,' I answered.

A moment later when I tried to change position, her voice came again: '*Mademoiselle*, are you OK? Just be still, don't be moving.'

After six days in hospital, I was discharged to the home of Jon Cadd, the pilot who had come to evacuate me. Jon and his wife, Cher, were kind and hospitable, opening their home also to Matthias and Sabine so that they could continue caring for me, looking after my dressings and intravenous drips. Jon loved animals and kept me amused with his numerous pets, including chameleons, snakes and a parrot which he had taught to drink Coca-Cola.

Any movement I made set off waves of pain, but medication to treat the pain made me nauseated and sleepy. Trying to work out why I was feeling so ill and weak, I asked the doctor to cut down the medication. I began to feel better and decided I would rather have pain than the dreadful nausea. Wives of some of the other MAF pilots showed me great kindness, helping with my personal care, doing my laundry and trying to tempt me with food. They made special juices for me to drink, brought me books, came and sat with me, and read and prayed. Through it all I was well looked after, surrounded by good friends and medical expertise. It was like having my own private hospital at home. On Sunday afternoon we sat outside listening to Jon playing his guitar. I was grateful to be alive and able to enjoy a time of fellowship with my friends.

I spent most of my days in an old canvas chair of Jon's, which I found comfortable despite the pain in my back. As the nausea subsided, Cher cooked me tasty meals. I also started doing some physio exercises and began to walk again. Dr Kibuka made the long journey from Bunia to visit me. It was lovely to see him and touching that he had gone to such effort to come.

Without the pain medication, I was not so sleepy and began to take an interest in some of the books my friends had kindly provided. When the incident came back into my mind, particularly when I woke at night, I tried to block it out, not wanting to relive the horror of that night. Sometimes reading helped to take my mind off my own situation as I followed the adventures of others.

I was particularly impressed by two books I read at Nyankunde. *Evidence Not Seen* by Darlene Deibler Rose is the story of a young American couple who served in Indonesia as missionaries with New Tribes Mission during the Second World War.[7] They were imprisoned by the Japanese in separate prisoner-of-war camps. When I read what that young wife suffered, and compared it to my own situation of love and care, I thought, 'What I'm suffering is mild in comparison. I have little to complain about.' It helped me to put everything in perspective and the happy ending cheered me greatly.

Another book I enjoyed was *The Help*, set in Mississippi in 1962 and an interesting study of black maids in a white world.[8] Coming from a background of living and working with Africans as colleagues, I found the whole topic gripping. Reading the book and watching the accompanying movie helped me forget about myself and was part of my recovery.

As I enjoyed this time of reading and reflection, I suddenly realised that the only chance I had had to read over many years was when I was unwell. In a normal day there was always too much to do to sit down and read a book. If I tried to read at bedtime, I would fall asleep. Even during my times back in Ireland I was always busy preparing for and speaking at meetings, keeping house, looking after the garden and visiting. I rarely set aside time just for myself. It was somewhat of a revelation.

This recuperation time also gave me a chance to look back and realise with gratitude how much I owed to MAF.

If it had not been for them, I could not have carried on the work I had done in Mulita over the years. Not only had they made this remote area accessible, but the pilots had become my friends and cared for me when I needed help. Set up seventy years ago by two young men with one little plane flying in Sudan, the organisation is now an international network flying more than 140 light aircraft to around 1700 destinations. I took time to thank God for the vision behind the whole organisation and the Christian love shown by their staff.

I realised again the truth of Paul's words to the Corinthians about the Christian family being the body of Christ: 'But God has put the body together … its parts should have equal concern for each other. If one part suffers, every part suffers with it; if one part is honoured, every part rejoices with it. Now you are the body of Christ, and each one of you is a part of it' (1 Corinthians 12:24–27). MAF staff had all used their various gifts as part of the ongoing work in Mulita as well as in the crises that had struck over the years. The shooting was just the latest in a long list of times when I needed them and they were there.

After five or six days with Jon and Cher, I was growing stronger and was transferred by MAF plane to Nebobongo, where Matthias and Sabine were based. One old lady who had been working in maternity when I first arrived in Nebobongo in 1968 was still there. She came to visit me in tears, thanking God that He had kept me alive. It was very humbling to see the love and concern of African brothers and sisters.

Word came that my second attacker had been apprehended. He had hidden for twenty-four hours in the forest off Mulita airstrip until the police search died down. Although he managed to get away, they found him later in Lubutu, 110 kilometres away. The man who had been caught first identified him.

I stayed in the Holmers' house in Nebobongo for another five weeks – until I was well enough to fly home. I missed Jon's comfortable old chair so I spent more time in bed, still unable to sit in an ordinary chair for any length of time. During those weeks people began arriving on their way through to the church general assembly meetings in Isiro which met every three years. They came with all their baggage on bicycles, including food for their time at the assembly: bananas, rice and peanuts. People had travelled hundreds of kilometres by bicycle to celebrate.

As I would normally have attended these meetings, MAF came to Nebobongo and flew me with Matthias and Sabine to Isiro. The church president wanted me to appear before the church for a short time to put paid to the rumours of my death. Sitting on the platform, I looked out over hundreds of faces, so many of whom had become dear friends over the years. As the president interviewed me, I shared the story of how God had saved my life. 'I am delighted to have this opportunity to thank you for your prayers,' I told the assembled crowd. 'I have no bitterness or revenge in my heart, just praise to God for what He has done for me. He will continue to be with us all whatever happens in the future.'

I had of course left Mulita with no preparation for departure. I was anxious to get back there to pack some things to take to Ireland and to leave instructions about the work in my absence. No one would agree to my going back to stay in Mulita for any length of time but I knew that at the end of the general assembly some church leaders would be flying back there. I made a quiet arrangement with the pilot to travel with them in order to pack up and hand over the work to others. The former Bible-school director from Mulita, Pastor Ikabu and his wife, Mama Idey, agreed to come with me. Having worked in Mulita, they knew people there and were happy to escort me.

I warned the pilot not to let anyone know I was going to Mulita. However word leaked out and by the time I arrived there a crowd was waiting to welcome me. A large vehicle arrived with the head chief, head of security and state administrator. It was gratifying that they were all anxious to see me and express their joy that I had survived the shooting, but as a result it was difficult to do any packing or handing over. Two hours disappeared very quickly before it was time to leave again.

Back in Nebobongo, I met Dr Francois who was going to take over the work in Mulita. Newly qualified and from the Mulita area, he would be an asset to the hospital. As I prepared to return to Ireland, I knew that God had the future of Mulita in His hands.

It had been a long process, but over the years of working in WEC International God had been making the core principles of the mission – faith, holiness, sacrifice and fellowship – a reality in my life. He had allowed me to experience fellowship with Christian believers from many backgrounds and nations. He had taught me to yield up everything I thought of as important, even my life, as a willing sacrifice. He was teaching me that my relationship with Him and His work in my life – changing me into His image – was the most important work of all. And each time I left the country, I continued to learn faith that He would care for those I left behind and that He would accomplish His purpose and build His church.

Two Irish missionaries, Jean Crooks and Amy Cuthbert, travelled from Ireland to meet me in Kampala and help me on my journey home. By this time I was feeling much better, but they had ordered a wheelchair which was a wonderful way to get through security in the various airports. To this day I do not know who booked the flights but I flew business class on the long-haul flight for the first and only time. It was a cold, wet day at the end of February when we arrived in Belfast but the welcome from my sister Margaret plus Jean's and Amy's husbands, Philip and Norman, warmed my heart.

18

IN THE SPOTLIGHT

The transition back into life in Ireland left me awestruck at God's care. A Christian medical consultant whom I had never met contacted me and offered his services. I accepted his kind offer. As he explained my scan results, he seemed as amazed as I was. 'You actually have two fractured ribs and two damaged vertebrae. The bullet went in through the front of your shoulder, missed a major artery and passed centimetres from your lung. It exited through your spine, partially destroying two of your vertebrae, but miraculously did not sever your spinal cord.' He examined the place where the bullet came out. There was still an open wound but it was healing well. God had kept me from bleeding to death or being paralysed.

Back home in Cookstown, Margaret dressed the wound every day as the fractures continued to heal. Sharing my story with others helped me think through what had happened. My attackers were doubtless aware that with no banks functioning in the country, I would have large amounts of cash in the house. However I realised that they had probably been expecting me to go out the front door of my house that night and I had wrong-footed them by using the back door. The more I thought about it, the more I realised that God had been in overall control of the whole situation.

I was taken aback by the publicity that surrounded my return to Ireland. My local church worked hard to shelter me, keeping my return date private. Rev. Ivor Smith, in charge while our normal minister was on leave, co-ordinated the publicity, doing preliminary interviews himself. When I felt strong enough to face the media, he arranged for all the interviews to take place in the church manse on one day.

A live interview by telephone with Stephen Nolan from Radio Ulster came first, after which television crews arrived from BBC and Ulster Television. A succession of journalists came from the *Belfast Telegraph*, *Belfast Newsletter* and a variety of local newspapers and ladies' magazines. I had not dreamt of the repercussions and opportunities that would result from the incident.

As I was presented with these openings to witness to God's power, I remembered Joseph's words to his brothers about the fact they had sold him into slavery: 'You intended to harm me, but God intended it for good' (Genesis 50:20).

I echoed them in my mind to the bandits: 'You have no idea how God is using your evil plot to bring glory to Him.' As a result of the situation, many people – who otherwise would not have heard – were presented with the miracles that God had done in DRC and in my life.

A few weeks later I received a telephone call from the *Belfast Telegraph*. The lady on the line sounded kind and asked how I was, before adding, 'I'm glad you're feeling better because I am telephoning to invite you to an awards ceremony in a hotel in Belfast. You have been nominated, along with a few others, for an award.'

'An award?' I was dumbfounded. 'What kind of award?'

'You have been nominated as Inspirational Woman of the Year 2015.'

I struggled to take it in. I had just been doing my normal day-to-day work in the place where God had called me. I could not understand why there was anything particularly inspirational about that. It was how Christians all over the world lived their lives. I responded, 'Oh no, I don't think I can go. That wouldn't really be my scene. I can't see myself travelling up to Belfast for that.'

'Well, we would love you to come. Please think about it and I'll be in touch again.'

Amused by the very idea, I shared the news of the invitation with my friends. David and Alana Millar from my home congregation encouraged me to go and offered to drive me. When I eventually agreed, my next problem was what I would wear. Not used to dressing up for special occasions, I had nothing suitable in my wardrobe. Then I remembered a dress that someone had passed onto me because it did not fit her any more. That would do fine.

Arriving at the venue, we were greeted by Wendy Austin from the BBC and other celebrities before being shown to our table. I began to relax and enjoy the meal as well as the company of the other guests. When the awards ceremony began, various categories were called, such as Mother of the Year and Teacher of the Year. I was hardly listening, not thinking I would feature. When I heard my name called as having won the award of Inspirational Woman of the Year, it came as a complete shock. At the prompting of my friends, I went forward in a daze to receive the award. I was used to working in a small Congolese village, far from any attention. This was well outside my usual sphere.

Having left the room for interviews and photographs, I returned to my friends at the table. By this time all the individual awards were completed and they were announcing a special overall award, Belfast Telegraph Woman of the Year. I had switched off from the main proceedings and was talking to the others at the table when I heard my name once more. I was so shocked I could not take it in. Again I made my way to the platform, this time for a more prestigious award. This was turning into a much bigger night than I had imagined.

The evening was full of surprises. One sponsor was Green & Black's from whom I received a wonderful collection of chocolate. The *Belfast Telegraph* gave me a bag of gifts. The Grand Opera House in Belfast gave me tickets to attend a show of my choice with guests. Sometime later I was able to treat my friends David and Alana to a night there in a VIP balcony, watching *The Sound of Music* together. Nothing had been further from my mind than all this when I was working day after day in Mulita.

The Nolan Show is a popular morning radio programme on Radio Ulster. Interviewing me on the show, Stephen Nolan asked, 'If your God is such a wonderful God, then why does He allow such a thing to happen to you?'

My reply was clear: 'Just as God was with Daniel in the lions' den, so He preserved my life in the face of that attack. He is more powerful than lions or bandits. When God showed His power in preserving Daniel's life, He left a challenge and encouragement to Christians all down the years. I feel that it has been a privilege to be in the lions' den, even to have been shot and at death's door, to prove God's delivering power. God knew what was happening and He is still in control.' Stephen Nolan may not have fully understood the basis for my confidence but my assurance of God's sovereignty had held me firm through good times and bad.

I had reason to make a quick recovery. With no postage service in DRC, my sister Margaret always opened my mail in Ireland. Just before Christmas in Mulita, I had received an email from her saying that a letter had come to Cookstown offering me an OBE in the Queen's New Year Honours. I thought she was joking; it took three emails before I was convinced that it was true. In the aftermath of the attack the whole matter faded to insignificance, but suddenly May and a trip to London were approaching. Goodbye Africa, welcome Buckingham Palace.

I was allowed to take three guests so I invited my sister Margaret who did so much for me, my niece, Pamela, and her husband, Allan. Pamela had been left with epilepsy after an attack of encephalitis and this was her first time flying since her illness. She was hesitant about going but we decided to trust God to keep His hand on the situation. The night before the investiture Pamela's sister arranged for us to have a meal together in a lovely London restaurant but Pamela had a bad seizure. Over the breakfast table the next morning we prayed that she would have no seizures during the ceremony.

Recipients of honours were welcomed to a drinks reception at the palace an hour before the event. There we were talked through the protocol for the investiture. It was fascinating to mingle and chat with the others, discovering the reasons for their various awards. Soon we were lined up in groups and escorted to the grand hall where we would receive our awards. I was naturally somewhat nervous but was conscious of the great privilege of being there.

As I stepped forward to receive my award, Prince William smiled. 'So you've been all over Africa?'

'No. Just the centre of Africa.'

There was sudden recognition in his face. 'Oh you're the lady who was shot.'

'Yes, that's right.'

'How are you now? Is the wound healing?'

'Yes, thankfully it is. I'm feeling much stronger.'

In a few minutes I received the award, reversed the required number of paces, curtseyed and walked off. The moment was over. It was a tremendous honour to be there but very humbling. I was conscious that it would never have happened but for my decision to follow the Lord almost sixty years before. Throughout those years I had depended on Him. I had also been supported by all those who had helped me to build the hospital and school as well as bringing about development in Mulita.

We went back to the hotel to change our clothes in preparation for our journey back to Ireland. Pamela had a series of seizures in the taxi, at the airport and on the plane home. We were grateful that God had answered our prayers and kept her well throughout the investiture ceremony.

It was a wonderful day. But up ahead there will be a far greater reward – one much more marvellous than Buckingham Palace – when we experience heaven's glory. The award I am looking forward to is seeing Jesus face to face and hearing the words 'Well done, good and faithful servant.'[9]

In September I was honoured to meet royalty again. Prince Edward, the Queen's youngest son, and his wife, Sophie, Countess of Wessex, hosted a garden party at Hillsborough Castle. Sheltering from the Irish rain under our umbrellas, Margaret and I explored the grounds and enjoyed afternoon tea in the marquee. I was one of the group of ladies selected to meet the Countess of Wessex while Prince Edward met some of the men. I found her pleasant and easy to talk to. As I was introduced as 'the lady who was shot in Congo', she was intrigued by my story and wanted to hear all the details.

September also brought a milestone for my friend Helen Roseveare as she celebrated her ninetieth birthday. With her health beginning to deteriorate, her friend Dr Pat Morton organised a quiet afternoon tea at their home for a few close friends. Helen cut the birthday cake and her rector, Rev. Tim Anderson, gave a heart-warming talk and prayed for her. It was always a delight to be with Helen and Pat in their home where they had supported each other over the years.

Helen, who had worked in Congo since 1953, moved back to the UK in 1973 to care for her mother, Lady Roseveare. After her mother's death, she visited Pat in Northern Ireland who, like Helen, was involved with the Girl Crusaders' Union. Helen settled in Northern Ireland where she and Pat were tireless in their commitment and service to the organisation in the UK, helping girls to know and love the God they served. In their earlier years together in Northern Ireland Helen helped Pat care for her mother until she died; in later years Pat cared for

Helen with great solicitude. Their home radiated the love of God and I continued to meet up with them during my times at home from Congo. Helen's international speaking and writing ministry persisted throughout her life.

Back in Mulita, despite the arrest of my two assailants, the authorities had also taken Onande, my night guard, and Aungala, the hospital secretary, into custody – two men whom I knew to be innocent. A month after the attack they had arrested Onande and fined him 150 dollars before releasing him. One month later they arrested him again and put him in prison. I was horrified at the news. I phoned the governor and the head of the army to assure them that Onande was completely innocent and that were it not for him I would have died. The governor had him released and he came back to guard my house. A few weeks later, however, he was rearrested. Tried in court, the jury gave an innocent verdict but the military continued to hold him. Meanwhile Aungala had been arrested almost immediately after the attack. When he had been in Punia the week before the attack, somebody said they saw him talking to one of the bandits, although the story was untrue.

Both men were taken to Kindu prison, where the real bandits were being held. In DRC prisoners are not fed unless relatives bring food, so prisoners can die of starvation. Fortunately Aungala was related to the chief in the area and a relative in Kindu arranged to bring food each day.

I was upset that these men had been arrested because of me and angry that the authorities ignored all evidence of their innocence. I tried to contact the governor again, phoning his residence in Kindu, but could not reach him. I contacted our church president and as many officials as possible. Eventually I managed to obtain temporary release for both of them but they were in great danger of being rearrested.

I decided that the only way I could sort this out was by going there in person. WEC were understandably reluctant for me to return, but I knew there was no other way to deal with the situation. Elizabeth Craig, a nurse whose parents had been missionaries in Congo and who had grown up there, offered to come with me. On 4 December 2015, eleven months after the attack, MAF flew us into Mulita once more.

I returned to a great celebration, with hundreds of people gathered at the airstrip to greet me as I stepped off the plane. A brass band played while the crowd waved and cheered at my arrival. I was so glad to see everyone and to be back among them. After exchanging greetings with local village and church leaders, Elizabeth and I were escorted through the village in a celebratory parade. The procession ended at a makeshift amphitheatre where a ceremony with singing, dancing and preaching was held in honour of my return.

After the ceremony, I returned to the airstrip to help unload the plane which was full of medical supplies and gifts I had brought from home. The main purpose of the trip, however, was to secure the permanent release of those who were being wrongly held. While Onande and Aungala had been the first to be arrested, Nelson, our head carpenter and church elder, was also under suspicion. Stories circulated, implicating a number of other people without foundation.

Some thought that the third man involved, whom I had never seen, was related to Nelson and had gone to his house on the verge of our compound that night. Local people said this was all untrue and I knew Nelson to be a godly Christian man who would on no account be part of any attack. Nonetheless the soldiers and police came after him, accusing him of being part of the plot. Threatened with arrest and imprisonment, he and his family went to hide in the forest. Then, because Nelson had disappeared, the authorities arrested his younger brother. John, his assistant, was also accused and imprisoned although he had nothing to do with the attack.

Nelson remained in the forest for months – all the time I was in Ireland. His wife was heavily pregnant when they went into hiding and gave birth to a baby girl. They called her after my niece, Pamela, for whom they had been praying since she became unwell in 2013. That really touched me and Pamela.

When I arrived back in Mulita, the man in charge of prisons and the main security person responsible for imprisoning those accused came to Mulita, where long discussions ensued. After listening to me, they responded, 'Yes, *Mademoiselle*, we understand what you are saying about the innocence of these men. We will deal with it.'

They went away but nothing happened. A week later I sent for them again and said, 'We need these men released and we need papers stating they are innocent. You said you would do something. Where are these papers?'

I knew they wanted money to produce the required documents. They knew I would not leave men suffering in prison without reason. It was a very difficult situation but yet again God used it for good. Aungala had undergone Bible-school training and done some preaching as an evangelist. He used his time in prison to talk to the other prisoners about Jesus and the Bible – in time they began to call him the pastor. As the months passed, he helped several prisoners put their trust in God.

Eventually the authorities relented. 'We see that you are speaking the truth about these people. They are innocent so they have been freed from prison. We have given them papers proclaiming their innocence so that they cannot be arrested again.'

I had achieved the main goal for my return to Mulita: the innocent men had been released. Details about the fate of the guilty men were vague but there was little I could do about them. Instead I turned my attention to the nursery school which we had started to build before I was attacked. Work had ceased with my departure so I organised the needed supplies and encouraged the builders to return to their task. I returned to Ireland at the end of January 2016, unsure when I would be back in Mulita but, as ever, committing the people and the work there into God's hands.

19

LOOKING FORWARD

'I feel the time has come to retire from my service with WEC International, with effect from January 2017.' In July 2016 I finally wrote the letter that had been hanging over me since my return from Mulita. I had served in DRC since 1968. I had been involved in Bible-school teaching and the training of Congolese nurses in two hospitals and several health centres. I had proved God's keeping power through epidemics, tropical storms and armed uprisings. I had returned after these events to rebuild and restart the work, an enduring love for the people of DRC driving me to help them medically and reach out to them spiritually. But at some point I had to acknowledge that my time there was coming to an end.

Before I retired, however, I was delighted to fly out to Mulita in October for one last visit as a WEC missionary. As soon as we had unpacked the much-appreciated medical supplies and other luggage, we concentrated on getting the pre-school nursery completed for the official opening ceremony on 11 November. That day the vehicle transporting the state administrator and his entourage of education officials broke down on the way from Punia, so the ceremony was delayed by four hours. However this was a blessing for me as I was ill with flu and was able to stay in bed until they arrived.

Other projects awaited us. We replaced the leaf roof on the head pastor's house with a corrugated tin roof, and built more mud houses for Bible-school staff and students, medical staff and primary-school teachers. We also replaced the rotten logs on the little bridge near Mulita. Before they left our area to work elsewhere in DRC, the German road company AAA gave us a large metal pipe to use instead. We managed to install it successfully, providing a more durable and reliable construction.

As well as supervising all this practical work, I was passing on my various streams of work to local helpers. I worked long hours completing Bible-school lessons to hand over to the Bible-school director. Maternity and pharmacy responsibilities I passed on to experienced and qualified personnel.

In November the state administrator arrived to see me and deliver a message: 'In July President Kabila carried out a visit to Maniema province. While he was in Kindu, he presented medals of honour to a number of people. He also left one for you in your absence.'

'The *Médaille du Mérite Civique*?' I was taken aback. 'But no expatriate ever receives this award.'

'That is true. No *mzungu* has ever received it before. But he wants to award it to you. The governor is asking you to go to Kindu to have it officially presented.'

'Well of course I am delighted to receive the medal. It is a great honour. But I am only here for two months and have so much to do. Also I have no transport to get there from Mulita. I will have to see what I can work out.'

The administrator departed, leaving me in a dilemma as to how I was to get to Kindu. Finally it was resolved: the MAF pilot who planned to fly me out of Mulita on 17 December kindly agreed a detour to Kindu so that the presentation ceremony could take place.

At the beginning of December Dr Listro, the eye consultant, made his annual visit to Mulita. As usual many people did not have the means to pay for their operation. Thankful for the generosity of friends in Ireland, I had the privilege of helping these patients and sharing in their joy at receiving their sight once more.

My departure date was drawing near when an incident occurred which almost jeopardised the planned presentation ceremony in Kindu. A church leader and his friends brought eight jerrycans of palm oil for me to buy, in an attempt to raise money for a new roof for their church. I had difficulty finding enough containers for the palm oil. The last container I found was not quite empty, containing what I assumed was paraffin oil. As I had watched the Congolese do many times, I put a struck match to the mouth of the container to disperse the fuel fumes. Unfortunately the contents turned out to be highly flammable aviation fuel and the ensuing ball of fire exploded over my right hand.

Grateful that it had not exploded in my face, I plunged my hand into a barrel of water. Nelson's wife, Maria, brought a basin of mud with which she proceeded to cover my hand, saying it would heal the wound, but the pain was unbearable. Reverting to the water treatment, I immersed it in ice-cold water from my solar-panel fridge, changing the water every half hour.

Seeing I was still suffering, Dominique, one of the nurses, appeared with a little jar of oil. 'Use this, *Mademoiselle.* It will help the pain.'

'What is it?' I was dubious.

'Snake oil. It is from the intestine of a snake found only in the Congo forest. It is very difficult to get.'

Willing to try anything, I applied some of the oil to my throbbing hand. Like a miracle cure, the pain disappeared. The burns took some time to heal but the worst of the pain had gone. I spent the rest of my time in DRC with my hand bandaged, curtailing my work somewhat, but with the opportunity to prove once again that God's grace is sufficient.

I knew the last week at Mulita would be busy with all the church leaders coming to say goodbye and Dr Listro being occupied with his eye patients. My Mulita farewell was marked by a feast which the medical staff had secretly arranged on the eve of my departure. It was a happy and joyful occasion, full of fun and laughter rather than sadness and tears. We gave thanks and praise to God for all His blessings over the years at Mulita.

On 17 December the MAF pilot collected Dr Listro and myself early in the morning so that we had time to fly to the provincial capital, Kindu, for my presentation ceremony and then on to Nyankunde in the afternoon. The local chief and two head pastors came with us from Mulita, planning to return by public transport. When we arrived in Kindu, however, the governor was attending an important funeral. Rather than cause offence by not accepting the *Médaille du Mérite Civique*, I wanted to wait for as long as possible.

Four hours later, the pilot and I decided we would have to leave, so the deputy governor proceeded with the ceremony. He presented me with the medal and delivered the appropriate speech: 'I wish to take this opportunity to thank you for all the development work you have done in Mulita and for your courage in coming back to DRC following the shooting.' I accepted the medal and accompanying certificate with gratitude.

We were just finishing when the governor arrived, apologising for the delay. Despite our attempts to leave, he insisted on repeating the ceremony, going through the entire process including pinning the medal onto my blouse.

It was now well into the afternoon and our pilot offered to fly the chief and pastors back to Mulita before continuing on to Nyankunde. People in Mulita were not expecting another plane that day, so a surprised crowd came running out when we appeared overhead. They had allowed cows onto the airstrip to graze, assuming it was not going to be used, and the final excitement of the day was trying to chase the animals away so that we could land. The pilot had to circle four times over the airstrip before it was cleared, by which time I was well and truly travel-sick. It was an ignominious end to a day of honour.

Back in Northern Ireland, on 7 December 2016, my dear friend and colleague Dr Helen Roseveare died at the age of ninety-one. I did not realise when I visited her before leaving Ireland that it would be for the last time. On 13 December her funeral service was held in the church she attended, St Elizabeth's Church in Dundonald, near Belfast. At the same time a memorial service was held for her in Nebobongo, where she had worked for so long.

Early in 2017 a service of celebration and thanksgiving for her life was held by WEC International in Bangor, Northern Ireland, which I had the privilege of not only attending but also opening in prayer. Dr Louis Sutton, International Director of WEC, came from Singapore to join John Bagg, the British director of WEC, and a representative from the Girl Crusaders' Union. Together they paid tribute to Helen and praised God for all that He had done through her. People around the world felt her loss; I had lost a personal friend.

Throughout 2017 I continued visiting churches in Northern Ireland which had supported the work in Mulita over the years. Towards the end of the year a measles epidemic in the Lowa and Mulita areas of DRC led to many infant deaths. I knew God wanted me to return once more with the medical supplies and equipment they so desperately needed.

I applied for a Congo visa early in December, sending off my passport to the embassy in London as usual. I bought my KLM plane ticket to Entebbe in Uganda for 15 January, and booked MAF flights to and from Mulita. Then I ordered the necessary medical supplies from JMS in Uganda and sent out heavy luggage ahead of my expected departure. One week before I was due to travel, my passport with the required visa had not returned from the embassy. I began to get concerned. Every day I prayed and watched for the postman, hoping it would come.

With no sign of the passport on Friday 12 January, I asked my good friend John Franklin to go to the embassy in London and retrieve it, even without a visa. With some difficulty he managed to obtain my passport and posted it to me by Royal Mail's Special Delivery on Friday afternoon. I waited expectantly on Saturday, but it did not arrive. In church on Sunday I shared prayer requests, especially for my passport and visa. Rev. Tom Greer asked the children to gather round me as they prayed specifically for these items. By Monday afternoon there was still no sign of them, and I was due to leave from Dublin Airport that night.

Dr Kibuka, who was working with immigration officials to try to obtain a visa in Goma, telephoned me that afternoon. 'I'm trying to get you a visa at this end,

Mademoiselle. Can you scan through a copy of your previous visa from last year? That would make it easier.'

'I'm sorry, I sent my passport to London for the visa and it has not come back. I have nothing here. If my passport doesn't come, I won't be able to travel.' I did not know what to suggest.

Just as I was speaking to him, the doorbell rang. I ran to the door with the phone in my hand and opened it to find the postman with my passport. In excitement I began to thank him. James Thompson, a church elder who had called round to help me, nudged me. 'Maud, you're still talking Swahili.'

'Oh, sorry,' I apologised to the postman. 'I'm talking to a friend in Congo.' I indicated the phone. 'Thank you so much for bringing this. You have no idea how grateful I am.'

The bemused postman left and Dr Kibuka, still on the phone, rejoiced with me for answered prayer. James scanned the visa and sent it immediately to Dr Kibuka. All I could do was praise God in the words of Jeremiah 32:17: 'Sovereign Lord … Nothing is too hard for you.'

Arriving in Uganda, I collected medical supplies and equipment, then travelled to the border at Goma. There immigration officials were pleasant but informed me they could only give me a visa for seven days. They assured me I would get a month-long visa in Mulita. As soon as I arrived there, I sent an official to Kindu with my passport to receive the correct visa. Once that was achieved, I was able to relax.

The measles epidemic had not ended. During my time there three children died while many others were being treated in hospital. Staff were overjoyed to receive the supplies I brought, which were essential to save these young lives. At the same time Dr Listro, the eye surgeon, had arrived in Mulita a few days before me and was able to help over 100 patients, operating on over sixty of them. As always I never ceased to be thrilled at the expression on the faces of those who had been totally blind but – when their bandages were removed – discovered they could see again.

On the two Sundays I was at Mulita I was asked to preach. There was a real sense of God's presence with us and His Spirit was at work in hearts and lives. I was thrilled that at the end of both services a large number of people came forward to give their lives to God. He was still working in this remote corner of Africa.

With my visa about to expire, I left Mulita and flew to Bunia, where I enjoyed a couple of days with MAF pilot Jon Cadd and his wife, Cher. I was full of thankfulness to God for enabling me to return to Mulita, for all He had done over the weeks I had been there and for this extra joy of meeting up again with kind friends and colleagues. I especially enjoyed time with Dr Kibuka and his wife, Alua. I returned to Ireland with a sense of completeness, knowing God was building His church in Mulita.

I started this work back in 1965, impelled by the voice of God to replace missionaries killed in the Simba rebellion. Over the years since then DRC has never really known peace. Although the Simbas were defeated, they regrouped to emerge in later years as community-based militia groups known as Mai-Mai, and then more recently the Raia Mutomboki. The First and Second Congo Wars, little more than a year apart, placed DRC at the centre of opposing African countries, where the powerless poor bore the brunt of the suffering. Between 1994 and 2003 it is estimated that five million people died as a result of the ongoing conflict.[10]

With over 200 tribes in the country, ethnic fighting rumbled on over the years, even when the major countries came to a peace agreement. In 2015 protests broke out across the country, with protestors demanding that Joseph Kabila step down as president. With his term due to expire in December 2016, elections were scheduled but were then postponed to 2018. Many have been arrested or lost their lives as protests and uncertainty continue. The UN peacekeeping force struggles to control the situation as millions are internally displaced, leading to large refugee camps, widespread disease and famine. DRC has vast mineral resources, rich soil and a favourable farming climate, but political instability, corruption and exploitation has reduced it over the years to one of the world's most needy countries.

Since the war, the tin mine at Tschamaka has almost ceased to function. These days it produces coltan, a valuable source of minerals used for mobile phones and electronic devices. It has been estimated that DRC has the world's largest reserves of coltan but looting, the departure of foreign investors and unregulated mining have resulted in many mines throughout the country being closed or reducing their output. Schools, hospitals, roads, the entire infrastructure needs investment.

And the people need God as much as they ever did. As an individual I can do little in the face of the overwhelming need. But over the years, with God's help, I have done what He has asked me to do. The situation in Mulita is very different to when I first arrived. A small clearing in the forest has now expanded into a hospital compound. This includes a maternity department, medical paediatric ward, surgical ward, operating theatre, outpatients department and administration block. The Bible school and church stand nearby, as do the primary and nursery schools. Housing for all the staff surrounds the main buildings.

Looking back over the years, I remember how rewarding it was to see the hospital built and the maternity department develop. As the primary- and nursery-school buildings took shape and the Bible school expanded, it was encouraging to see qualified staff taking responsibility. Local people who left to go to school and university have returned equipped to take over the work, some as teachers for the school and one even as a doctor for the hospital. Seeing African evangelists going out from the Bible school in Mulita to start up new churches and become pastors never fails to thrill me. Watching the church grow over the years, not just in numbers but in depth and spirituality, reminds me that despite the setbacks, God's promise still holds true: 'I will build my church; and all the powers of hell shall not prevail against it' (Matthew 16:18, TLB).

The promises of God have upheld me throughout everything that has happened in my life. The longer I know Him and the more experiences I go through, the deeper my understanding that God is sovereign. When my bungalow in Cookstown was burgled, when I was shot in Mulita and when I was evacuated from Congo because my life was in danger, God reminded me, 'I'm in control here.' In the midst of crisis, God was near. He is in control of everything that happens. When we truly believe this, it brings great peace.

God first called me to Congo with the words: 'I have placed before you an open door that no one can shut' (Revelation 3:8). At the outset that door appeared closed, and many times over the years the door closed again. But God always reopened it. He kept His hand on the open door so that I could follow His call and He could continue His work in that place.

Now that I spend most of the year back in Ireland, I have to release the work in Mulita into the hands of those coming after me. I call to mind the words from the traveller's psalm: 'The Lord will keep your going out and your coming in from this time forth and forevermore' (Psalm 121:8, ESV). I would often read this when setting out to go back to DRC. Those words are as true for me today as they were when I was in Congo. He will care for me in Ireland as in DRC. He will care for the Congolese church as He does for the church in the UK.

At the outset of my missionary journey, I knew that I was called to suffer as Christ suffered for us: 'rejoice … as you participate in the sufferings of Christ, so that you may be overjoyed when his glory is revealed' (1 Peter 4:13). At that stage I had no idea exactly what this would mean. But I look back now and rejoice for the limited ways in which I shared His suffering. What an honour to identify with Him, trivial though my experience was in comparison to what He did for us. When we deny ourselves, take up the cross and follow Him, we are saying we are willing for whatever that entails. It is an adventure. Following Jesus – walking with Him – when we do not know where He will lead us, is the most exciting life.

Thinking of what God has done in Mulita over the years, I return to verses He gave me many years ago: 'Brothers and sisters, think of what you were when you were called. Not many of you were wise by human standards; not many were influential; not many were of noble birth. But God chose the foolish … the weak … the lowly … the despised … so that no one may boast before him ... Therefore, as it is written, "Let the one who boasts boast in the Lord"'(1 Corinthians 1:26–31).

He has done it all. All glory belongs to Him.

NOTES

1. The *chef de poste* is the pastor's assistant, responsible for the smooth running of mission stations.

2. Winnie's full story can be read in *The Captivity and Triumph of Winnie Davies* by David M. Davies (Hodder & Stoughton, 1967).

3. See Matthew 6:6.

4. The *Jesus* film is a docudrama on the life of Christ that was produced in 1979, has been translated into 1400 languages and is used worldwide as an evangelistic tool.

5. Helen Roseveare, *Digging Ditches* (Christian Focus, 2005).

6. All church groups had to be members of one basic Protestant church in Congo, with each denomination or mission identified by a number. WEC churches were known as CECCA16 –

Communauté Evangélique du Christ au Coeur de L'Afrique.

7. Darlene Deibler Rose, *Evidence Not Seen* (HarperCollins, 1988).

8. Kathryn Stockett, *The Help* (Penguin, 2009).

9. See Matthew 25:23.

10. See www.bbc.co.uk/news/world-africa-13283212

'THIS IS A STORY YOU NEED TO READ. I HAVE BEEN STIRRED AND BLESSED BY IT.'
AN OPEN DOOR
A TRUE STORY OF COURAGE IN CONGO
MAUD KELLS
WITH JEAN GIBSON
PATRICIA ST JOHN'S STORY